The Letters of John

THE
LETTERS
OF
JOHN

BY

DALE MOODY

WORD BOOKS, Publishers
Waco, Texas—London, England

Living Word
Christian Center

To

ROBERT B. HENSLEY

"that we may be fellow-workers in the truth"

III John 8

PREFACE

Over a period of many years I have returned to the letters of John for expository preaching and out of historical interest for their place in Christian origins. An exposition has been promised so many times that a credibility gap has no doubt been created, but here it is at last.

It is my conviction that one of the great needs of the churches today is biblical preaching based on historical exposition. There needs to be no rift between the most exacting historical research and the relevant application to personal and social issues. One would think that B. F. Westcott dispelled that doubt in the last century. It was the commentaries of this great scholar and saint that first deepened my interest in the Johannine writings. The research from Westcott to Rudolf Schnackenburg and Rudolf Bultman has indeed been enormous, but Westcott remains a model. The most original work in between was perhaps that by C. H. Dodd.

I am well aware that Westcott was Anglican and Dodd is Congregational, that Schnackenburg is Catholic and Bultmann is Lutheran, and this enables me to say that exegetical exposure in broad dialogue is the soundest way toward a biblical foundation for Christian understanding. This is no time to listen only to those of one school of thought. It is symbolic that this little book was written in the midst of Christian encounters in Asia and Europe.

The dedication is to a beloved Louisville layman who has made Acts 20:35 more believable ("It is more blessed to give than to receive"). On more than one occasion he has been my generous Gaius to enable me to travel to Turkey and other remote places in the interest of the apostolic faith found in the New Testament. It was as great a thrill to be in Ephesus in the midst of this writing as it was to be in Rome while I wrote my commentary on Paul's letter to the Romans.

Dr. Harold Smith, pastor of Davis Memorial Baptist Church in

Louisville, checked my manuscript for errors. Dr. Peter Rhea Jones of Southern Seminary did the same for the galley pages. To each of them I am truly grateful, not only for their help but for their warm friendship.

May the readers of this brief commentary experience the light, life, and love revealed in Jesus Christ who was made more real to the writer as the words were writen. Never before has the incarnation of God in the flesh of Jesus Christ become so central for my personal faith. Indeed, "this is the victory that overcomes the world, our faith" (I John 5:4).

Dale Moody
June 1, 1970

Contents

Chapter 1

INTRODUCTION TO THE LETTERS OF JOHN

Stage of New Testament Revelation

The writings of the New Testament may be compared to a building with five floors. On the first floor are the teachings of the historical Jesus which are included in the Four Gospels. The second floor is occupied by the Palestinian churches, especially the church of Jerusalem, and some of the teachings of the mother church may be found by a careful study of the Acts of the Apostles, especially chapters 1-12. Hellenistic Jewish Christianity, i.e. Jewish Christianity that spoke Greek and was more influenced by Greek culture, lives on the next floor. It is not always easy to discover the teachings on this third level, but the letters called James, Peter, and Jude, together with Hebrews, may be considered rooms. Many teachings which belong to this level are to be found in the Pauline and Johannine collections. The Pauline writings are in general the room for Gentile Christianity.

The Johannine collection of writings, i.e. all the writing associated with the name of John, are Gentile also, but there is an interesting blend of the Jewish and Gentile types set in opposition to the heretical movement known as Gnosticism. It will be noted that these writings in the Ephesian area have the closest connections with the pre-Christian Jewish writings discovered

11

after 1947 at Qumran. This may be designated the fifth and final floor of the New Testament revelation, since the high Christology of pre-existence and incarnation found in the Pauline writings is also related to the historical Jesus. Paul wrote no Gospel, so it is not possible to speak with assurance as to how he saw the historical Jesus. In the Gospel of John the historical Jesus and the preexistent Son of God are seen in the light of the death and resurrection of Jesus Christ. On the basis of this complete Christology, the letters of John were written.

Place in the New Testament Canon

There are two major views regarding the authorship of the Johannine writings in the Greek tradition. Clement of Rome, in his letter to Corinth, A.D. 95, twice used the phrase "made perfect in love" (I John 4:18, cf. 2:15). In Asia, Polycarp of Smyrna, about A.D. 108, quoted I John 4:2 with echoes of I John 2:24; 3:8. Papias of Hierapolis, about A.D. 140, according to Irenaeus, used the phrase "the truth itself" (cf. III John 12). All these are free from any question of the apostolic origin of the Johannine writings.

The most important authority for the apostolic origin of the Johannine writings is Irenaeus of Lyons, who came from Asia and later worked in Gaul. He knew only one John of Ephesus, "the disciple of the Lord, who also had leaned on his breast" (Against Heresies, III.I.I), who lived until the time of Trajan, A.D. 98-118 (III.iii.4). His knowledge was perhaps derived from Polycarp, who was instructed by the apostles and whom Irenaeus knew in his early youth (III.iii.4). Polycarp is the only link between Irenaeus and the apostle John.

The Muratorian Canon, from the Italian Muratori who discovered it, is a document in barbarous Latin that is believed to be based on a Greek original by Hippolytus from the end of the second century. It attributes the Gospel of John to the same "John, one of the disciples" in much the same way as Irenaeus. I John 1:1 is quoted and two letters "bearing the name of John" are mentioned. Which "two" letters is uncertain.

The tradition is mixed in Alexandria and Antioch. Clement of Alexandria, about A.D. 140, knew two letters of John also and quotes I John freely. Origen, according to Eusebius, knew of "a second and a third" letter of John, but he reports the doubt about their genuineness (*Church History* VI.25.10). Dionysius of Alexandria, a pupil of Origen, had a dislike for Revelation, but he held the apostolic authorship of John and I John (*Church History* VII.25-26). The famous Easter Letter by Athanasius of Alexandria in A.D. 367 traced all the Johannine writings to the apostle.

These doubts about II and III John and the Revelation were embraced and defended by Eusebius of Caesarea, about A.D. 325. The Alexandrian tradition to which he belonged had a strong dislike for the eschatology in II John and Revelation, particularly the chiliasm that prevailed in Asia. (Chiliasm, from the Greek *chilia*—a thousand—was a belief that Christ would return and rule on earth a thousand years. In general, the church fathers of Asia Minor accepted this view, while those from Alexandria rejected it.) This was almost certain to color his views on the apostolic authorship of II, III John, and Revelation (*Church History* III.39.6). John Chrysostom in the fourth century and Theodore of Mopsuestia in the fifth, also of the Antioch school, made no use of II and III John as canonical Scripture. The Syrian Canon of the fifth century, called the Peshitta, has only three general letters (James, I Peter, I John).

In the Latin writers, the Mommsen Canon of about A.D. 360, from the German who discovered it, says there are 3,350 verses (i.e., lines) in the "letters of John," but someone has written "only one" underneath. Jerome of Bethlehem, the translator of the Latin Vulgate, agreed with all the rest on the apostolic authorship of John and I John, but he reports the tradition about two men named John in Ephesus (*De Viris Illustribus*, 9, 18). The Council of Carthage of A.D. 397, attended by Augustine, adopted the views of Athanasius of Alexandria.

This view prevailed in the West until modern scholarship revived the ancient doubts not only in regard to II, III John, and Revelation but of John and I John as well. C. H. Dodd is representative of those who not only reject the apostolic authorship of all the Johannine writings but would have as many as three non-apostolic authors: the author of John, the author of the three letters, and the author of Revelation. Recent investigations into the role of secretaries and the influence of Qumran, together with the importance of chronological development, tend to put Irenaeus in a better light than modern scholarship has thought.. It just could be that as many as three secretaries were used, but the tradition seems apostolic.

The Historical Situation

The traditional view, based mostly on Irenaeus, dated the Johannine writings in the last decade of the first century and attributed them to the apostle John. The following commentary has led to much the same conclusions, although the new knowledge from Qumran puts this in a very different light. The role of private secretaries and chronological order must also be considered in matters of style. In general the order of the Johannine writings seems to be: the Revelation, the first edition of the Gospel, the three letters in the canonical order, then the final edition of the Gospel with the prologue (1:1-18), the epilogue (ch. 21), and certain emendations added.

All of these writings reflect a growing resistance to a form of Gnostic Judaism! This is not a slip. Gnostic Judaism may be found in the writings of Qumran, and this was in some unknown way brought to Asia. This mixture of Judaism and Gnosticism at some times rejected the belief in Jesus as the Christ (Judaism) and at other times the belief that the Son of God really became flesh (Gnosticism). The two beliefs, in different ways, denied the incarnation, but they often merge. It is not surprising that Irenaeus classifies the Jewish Ebionites with the Gnostics (*Against Heresies.* I.XXVI.2). Details are in the commentary. Justin Martyr later reflected this movement in his own spiritual pilgrimage from Judaism through Greek philosophy to orthodox Christianity.

Respect for the accuracy of Irenaeus of Lyons and reservations about the theories of Eusebius of Caesarea have been increased by a new look at these letters in the light of recent discoveries both before and after the date of the Johannine letters. The discoveries of forty-nine Gnostic writings at Nag-Hammadi in Egypt (1945-1946) alter the picture presented by the anti-Gnostic church fathers very little (Justin, Irenaeus, Hippolytus, Tertullian). A very balanced view of this fact is provided by R. M. Grant in his article on "Gnosticism" in *The Interpreter's Dictionary of the Bible.* The special relationship between I John and Qumran has been explored in a novel way by J. C. O'Neill's work on *The Puzzle of*

I John (S.P.C.K., 1966), but this has been used with reservations.

Gnosticism is the most general term applied to the heresy refuted by the letters of John. The name is derived from its concern with *gnosis* (mystical knowledge). This term is used primarily to designate the dualism between God and matter that led to a denial of a good creation, a real incarnation, and the resurrection of the body. The special application to the incarnation is often called Docetism, from *dokein* (to seem), because it taught that Jesus only *seemed* to be a real human being with flesh and blood. The chief representative of the Gnostic heresy in Ephesus was a certain Cerinthus who claimed that the Christ descended upon Jesus at his baptism but flew back to the Unknown Father before Jesus died on the cross (Irenaeus, *Against Heresies* I.XXVI.I).

Literary Style

A very close connection in literary style exists between the three letters of John and the Gospel. Even though the Gospel has a more developed realized eschatology than that of the letters, all of them have retained some of the futurist eschatology in the Revelation (John 6; I John 2:18-3:3; 4:1-6; II John 7). The Christology of incarnation is very much the same in the letters and the Gospel, and it is only in regard to developing institutionalism that II and III John go beyond I John. Neither John nor I John give the name of an author, but II and III John claim to be from "the elder." II John is mysteriously addressed to an elect lady that is almost sure to be a church, but III John is addressed to a beloved member of a divided church. It is only in Revelation that the author is called John (1:1,9). Apocalypse, Gospel, a letter that is near to an epistle, and two ordinary letters compose the Johannine corpus.

The literary structure of I John is much like the Meander River in Asia where such teachings were first formulated against the Gnostic threat. The twisting and turning of the Meander became proverbial. Hence, the English verb "to meander." Some have thought the repetitions of themes in I John impossible to outline, but this is hardly true when the three cycles with four subheads are seen. I John really picks up volume as new thoughts pour in like tributaries into the Meander. At first a stream of *light* is fed by the four tributaries of avoiding sin, keeping the commandments, overcoming the world, and guarding against the enemy of faith. It meanders on as the last two tributaries are merged in one channel, and the stream of *light* becomes a river of *life*. Before the end the major channel becomes the commandment of *love*, but the other three can still be distinguished. The outline and commentary illustrate and interpret this development. Most of I John is Hebrew poetry but only a few lines in II and III John have this quality. Therefore, my own translation is made of I John, but the *Revised Standard Version* has been followed in the last two.

The other two letters are supplements to the first and presuppose its contents. It is possible that II John was written last, but it is left in the traditional order. II John speaks of the church with the mysterious metaphor of a chosen lady, but III John is a straightforward letter to a beloved Gaius who seems the only hope against a domineering Diotrephes. It is the ecclesiology of the last two letters that goes beyond the Christological concern of the first. When the more ethical teachings in the letters of John are combined with the apocalyptic vision of the future, the second coming of Christ, in the Revelation, and the dramatic interpretation of the first coming of Christ, in terms of the Jewish feasts, in the Gospel, a very complete version of Christianity according to John emerges. It is the great watershed between the apostles and the fathers. It is altogether possible that II, III John were covering letters sent forth with copies of I John. I John was a general letter.

Outline of the First Letter of John

PROLOGUE (1:1-4)

I Light (1:5-2:27).
   1. The theme (1:5).
   2. Avoiding sin (1:6-2:2).
      (1) Sin and fellowship (1:6-10).
      (2) Sin and forgiveness (2:1-2).
   3. Keeping the commandments (2:3-11): obedience.
      (1) The commandments and knowledge (2:3-6).
      (2) The commandment and love (2:7-11).
   4. Overcoming the godless *kosmos* (2:12-17).
      (1) The blessings of the *koinōnia* (2:12-14).
      (2) The lusts of the godless *kosmos* (2:15-17).
   5. Guarding against the enemy (2:18-27): antichrists.
      (1) The antichrists are those who depart from the *koinōnia* (2:18-21).
      (2) The antichrists are those who deny that Jesus is the Christ (2:22-25).
      (3) The antichrists are those who would deceive the anointed (2:26-27).

II Life (2:28-4:6).
   1. Avoiding sin (2:28-3:10a).

17

   (1)   The preparation of God's children for the *parousia* (2:28-3:1).

   (2)   The purification of God's children before the *parousia* (2:2-6).

   (3)   The manifestation of God's children before the *parousia* (3:7-10a).

  2. Keeping the commandments (3:10b-24).

   (1)   The commandment and the brother (3:10b-18).

   (2)   The commandments and God (3:19-24).

  3. Guarding against the enemy in the godless *kosmos* (4:1-6): false prophets.

III Love (4:7-5:21).

  1. Keeping the commandment (4:7-21): love.

   (1)   Manifested love (4:7-11).

   (2)   Abiding love (4:12-16).

   (3)   Perfect love (4:17-18).

   (4)   Brotherly love (4:19-21).

  2. Overcoming the godless *kosmos* (5:1-13): faith.

   (1)   The triumph of God's children (5:1-5).

   (2)   The testimony of God (5:6-13).

  3. Avoiding sin (5:14-17): prayer.

  4. Guarding against the enemy (5:18-21): knowledge.

Outline of the Second Letter of John

I Salutation (1-3).

II Following the commandment: *entolē* (4-6).

III Guarding against the deceivers: *didachē* (7-11).

IV Conclusion (12-13).

Outline of the Third Letter of John

I Salutation to Gaius (1-4).

II Cooperation of Gaius (5-8).

III Opposition of Diotrephes (9-10).

IV Exhortation and Recommendation of Demetrius (11-12).

V Conclusion (13-15).

Chapter 2

COMMENTARY ON THE FIRST LETTER OF JOHN

THE PROLOGUE (1:1-4).

1 That which was from the beginning,
which we have heard,
which we have seen with our eyes,
which we have looked upon
and touched with our hands,
concerning the Word of Life—

2 And the life was manifested,
and we have seen,
and we are bearing witness,
and we are proclaiming to you
the eternal life which was with the Father
and was manifested to us—

3 that which we have seen and heard we are proclaiming to you,
in order that you may have fellowship with us;
and our fellowship is with the Father
and with his Son Jesus Christ;
4 and these things we are writing to you,
in order that *our* joy may be complete.

A prologue proclaims at the very beginning the theme of a writing. II John and III John begin with salutations, as in all the Pauline letters, but all the other Johannine writings begin with a powerful prologue. An obvious connection exists between the prologue of I John and John. Both use the phrase at the beginning of Genesis ("The beginning," Genesis 1:1; I John 1:1; John 1:1). Words such as Word, Father, life, witness are met in both prologues. There are, however, some differences. In I John the Word is not yet personified as in the Gospel, and it is really the life that is manifested rather than the Word. The prologue of the Gospel gives the appearance that it is a later development of the themes sounded in the prologue of I John, and this makes the earlier writing very important for understanding the more elaborate developments in the Gospel, and the Gospel important for understanding the direction of the Letter.

The prologue speaks first of what became known as the incarnation of life (1:1). Life (zoe) is always eternal life, God's life that comes out of eternity into time and is mediated to men by the Word. "That which was from the beginning" means that which was when all things began. This is clearly the meaning of "the beginning" when he speaks of "him who is from the beginning" (2:13, 14), but it is perhaps the meaning even when he speaks of "an old commandment which you had from the beginning" (2:7), "what you heard from the beginning" (2:24), and "the message which you have heard from the beginning" (3:11). The commandment and the message are the eternal truth that comes from God. Of course this includes "the beginning of the gospel" with the preaching of John and Jesus (cf. Mark 1:1), but the Johannine writings have moved beyond the first stage anchored to apostolic history to the second stage, which does not exclude the first, that anchors the gospel in eternity. I John is the beginning of the Johannine teaching on the preexistence of the Son that bursts forth with glorious light in the Gospel.

A gospel anchored in both eternity and history makes it necessary to develop a doctrine of incarnation by which the eternal is united to the historical: "And the Word became flesh" (John 1:14). To use the term of the modern cameraman, John "zooms in on" the incarnation. However, he zooms down, not up, for he starts in eternity and moves at blinding speed from sound to sight, from seeing to looking at close range, to actual touching or handling with the hands. In one mighty dive he destroys both incipient Gnosticism which would despise and deny the flesh and the elementary Christology of the Ebionites who would reduce the person of Christ to no more than the son of Joseph and Mary on whom the Holy Spirit in the form of a dove came at Jesus' baptism. It is amazing how both alternatives to the incarnation have a fascination for superficial Christology today.[1]

The Word of life could be printed *the word of Life,* for it is life that is personified as in John 1:4 ("and the life was the light of men"). The Word or word is the historical event by which the eternal life of God is disclosed. The combination of word and life is found elsewhere in the New Testament only in Philippians 2:16 ("holding fast the word of life"), where the meaning is the gospel, but the Johannine phrase means more than that. Logos in the Johannine writings has inherited meanings both Hebraic and Hellenistic. In the Old Testament the Word of the LORD was the medium of both revelation and creation (Isaiah 2:3; 55:10-11; Psalm 33:6). This was also the meaning of the Word of God (Genesis 1, "God said—God called; God said—God made," etc.). The Wisdom of the LORD is another term that expressed God's revealing and creative action (Proverbs 8:22-31). Philo prepared the way for the Johannine usage by uniting the Hebrew heritage to the Stoic concept of Logos as the immanent principle that gave meaning to the universe. The Gospel of John speaks both of the words *(rhēmata)* that gave life (6:68) and of the collective *Logos* that gathers all *rhēmata* together as Truth (17:6-8, 14, 17). The seeds of these are sown in I John.

Life is a twofold concept in I John. At times it is *bios,* that which constitutes earthly life or the means by which earthly life is sustained (2:16; 3:17). This is life in a quantitative sense, but *zoe,* the other Greek word used for life, has a qualitative meaning that almost makes the adjective "eternal" unnecessary. It is the very life of God mediated through the incarnate and historical word. The Gospel of John heightens the meaning of *zoe* even more and does not even use the word *bios.* This radical distinction

---

[1] Cf. John Knox, *The Humanity and Divinity of Jesus* (Cambridge University Press, 1967).

is not brought out in words like biology and zoology. *Zoe* must be understood in the Johannine context.

The manifestation of life is an elaboration of the idea of incarnation (1:2). It is difficult to bring out the full meaning of the Greek tenses in translation. In verse 1 two perfect tenses are followed by two aorists. The perfect tense brings out the permanent significance of sound and sight, while the aorist indicates the point of action of the personal experience of looking and touching. "Manifestation" in verse 2 is brought out with the aorist tense at the beginning and the end with one perfect and two present tenses in between. This means that the manifestation was a definite point in history for which there are eyewitnesses to transmit it through history. It is this horizontal transmission of eternal truth that gives meaning to the idea of manifestation. God has disclosed his truth in actual historical events in an actual historical person. The present tenses of witnessing and proclaiming express the continuation of this historical transmission of truth. The Eternal Life and the Logos of Life are the same, and the statement that the eternal life was "with the Father" before manifestation is further evidence that "from the beginning" implies preexistence.

The Father is John's favorite term for God (1:2,3; 2:1,14,15, 16,22,23(2); 3:1; 4:14). Even in the Old Testament God is rarely called Father (Isaiah 63:16; 64:8; Psalm 89:26). The coming of Jesus into the world gave a new meaning to God's Fatherhood, for Jesus not only called God Father himself, but he taught his disciples to do the same (Mark 14:36; Matthew 6:9). The so-called low Christology of the Synoptic Gospels that says nothing about preexistence and incarnation lays the foundation for the high Christology of John's Gospel that interprets even the historical Jesus in the light of preexistence and incarnation. The beginnings of this Logos Christology are found in such expressions as "from the beginning" and "which was with the Father." These are not two contradictory Christologies but two stages in a complete Christology anchored in history.

The proclamation of the incarnate and manifested life is the way to fellowship (1:3). For the third time the perfect tense for "hearing" and "seeing" is used, this time in the reverse order of "seen" and "*heard*." For the second time he says "we are proclaiming," the present tense of perpetual witnessing to the truth. The purposes of the proclamation introduced a term for which there is no adequate translation. At times *koinōnia* is translated "communion," but this has become too narrow in meaning. At other times it is translated "fellowship," but this has become too broad and flat. In Luke 5:10 the joint owners of a fishing fleet are called *koinōnoi,* and this suggests some meaning such as partnership. In good Western slang a Christian may well be addressed as "pardner!"

This partnership or fellowship is first of all human ("that you may have fellowship with us"). Christianity is as human as it is historical. The absence of the human is as much heresy as the absence of the historical. Any claim of vital relationship with God that is not manifested in genuine human fellowship is a pious fraud. It is the absence of this human side of fellowship that has driven many, all too many, from the temple to the tavern. The word *koinōnia* is the Johannine word for what Paul called the body of Christ, the church. Belonging to the fellowship would be a good way to describe New Testament membership in the church. There people could find love and express love, and as they did, they found God and experienced God. What a far cry from the sophisticated superiority that speaks of a congregation gathered for worship as "the crowd."

Human meetings may also be empty. People can be in the same place like marbles in a barrel. Genuine human fellowship has as its foundation that heavenly fellowship "with the Father and with his Son Jesus Christ." This is the Christian unity for which Jesus prayed in the High Priestly Prayer of John 17:21 ("that they may all be one; even as Thou, Father, art in me, and I in thee, that they also may be in us, so that the world may believe that thou hast sent me"). The Father-Son relationship is not only the first step toward the doctrine of the Holy Trinity; it is also the model for fellowship among the disciples of Jesus.

The Sonship of Jesus is a corollary to the Fatherhood of God. Paul can speak of Jesus as Son and believers as sons, but John reserves the word Son for Jesus. When he speaks of believers in this relation to God, he uses such terms as "children," "little children," and "young children," never the term "sons." The *Authorized (King James) Version* is in error on John 1:12. The

sonship of Jesus to God the Father has many implications, but the
obedience of Jesus to the Father's will and the love of the Father
for the Son are always present. As a model for Christian fellowship, this eternal relationship calls for obedience to the commandment of love.

The last two lines (1:4) bring the authorship and the purpose
of the Letter into full focus. The frequent use of "we," "his," and
"our" raises the question of who are "we." Is it an editorial "we"
for the author himself? The "we write" on the one hand and
"you" on the other supports the view that two groups are in mind.
C. H. Dodd and Amos N. Wilder are perhaps correct in seeing
this as an expression of a Christian solidarity that would include
all believers. Some later references can hardly be restricted to
the author or even to the apostolic witnesses. "By this we know
that we abide in him and he in us, because he has given us of his
own Spirit. And we have seen and testify that the Father has sent
the Son as the Savior of the world" (4:13-14). The Gospel of
John speaks in the same way ("we have beheld his glory . . .
from his fullness have we all received," 1:14,16).

The purpose of the Letter is the completion of joy in the fellowship. Some manuscripts have "your joy," but the strongest evidence
is for "our joy." The completion of joy is the completion of the
fellowship, for the fruit of fellowship is joy. The Pauline Body
of Christ is the Johannine Vine. As the branches abide in the Vine
and bear fruit, more fruit, and much fruit, the joy of fellowship
becomes complete. "These things I have spoken to you, that my
joy be in you, and that your joy may be full" (John 15:11. Cf.
16:24; 17:13).

Chapter 3

COMMENTARY ON THE FIRST LETTER OF JOHN

LIGHT (1:5—2:27).

1. The theme (1:5)

> This is the message
> > which we have heard from him
> > > and we are announcing to you,
>
> that God is light
> > and in him is no darkness at all.

A dozen more declarations are found in I John. Three of them repeat themes (3:11, 23; 4:3), but three summarize whole sections (1:5; 2:25; 4:21). Seven are found in the final summary of our faith (5:3,4,6,9,11,14,20). This declaration is followed by two parallelisms, the first synthetic and the second antithetic. The perfect tense for "hearing" appears for the third time, but this time it is said to be "from him." It is usually assumed that "him" means Jesus. *Today's English Version (Good News for Modern Man)* takes the liberty to translate "from his Son," but this is not at all sure. In 1:1,3 the Son of God is the one about whom they have heard through the apostolic witness, and there is no good reason to take a different approach here. It is now about God that they have heard, but the teacher is still the witness.

The announcement is one of the two metaphors for God in I John: "God is light" (1:5) and "God is love" (4:14,16). God as life is implicit in the metaphor for God as "spirit" (John 4:24), but it is not found in I John's teaching on the nature of God or the Holy Spirit. Cf. I John 2:29 for God as righteous.

Light is often associated with God in the Old Testament. God created the light as good (Genesis 1:3). "The LORD is my light and my salvation" (Psalm 27:1) and "In thy light shall we see light" (Psalm 36:9) are examples that have had great influence in Christian civilization. *The Manual of Discipline* at Qumran said: "The origin of truth lies in the Fountain of Light, and that of perversity in the Wellspring of Darkness. All who practice righteousness are under the domination of the Prince of Lights, and walk in the ways of light; whereas all who practice perversity are under the domination of the Angel of Darkness and walk in ways of darkness" (3:18). Philo said: "God is light, and not light only, but the archetype of every other light, or rather more ancient and higher than any archetype" (*On Dreams* 1.75). Echoes of this type of thinking are heard in I John. God is light but not all light is God. God is "the Father of lights" (James 1:17).

The sections on light may be gathered around four subordinate topics: avoiding sin (1:6-2:2), keeping the commandments (2:3-11), overcoming the godless *kosmos* (2:3-17), and guarding against the enemy (2:18-27).

2. Avoiding sin (1:6-2:2).

This is brought out in the following arrangement and translation:

> 6 If we go about saying that "we are having fellowship with him"
> and we are walking about in the darkness,
> we are lying and we are not doing the truth.

> 7 But if we are walking about in the light
> as he is in the light,
> we are having fellowship with him
> (and the blood of Jesus, His Son, makes us clean from all sin).

8 If we go about saying that "we have no sin,"
  we are deceiving ourselves
    and the truth is not in us.

9 (If we go about confessing our sins,
  he is faithful and righteous
    and will forgive our sins
      and cleanse us from all unrighteousness).

10 If we go about saying that "we have not sinned,"
  we are making a liar out of him
    and his word is not in us.

(1) Sin and fellowship (1:6-10). Pseudo-religion, religion that lives a lie *(pseudos)*, claims to have fellowship with God without cleansing from sin. It is put in contrast to genuine religion that finds in Jesus the Paraclete the true remedy for sin. Pseudo-religion is portrayed in four stanzas of poetry, with three lines each, and this is perhaps an early Christian hymn of the type found in the Qumran writings called *The Hymn of the Initiants* and *The Book of Hymns*. In the background is the praise of God in the many Psalms, not only in the Psalter, but in the whole of the Old Testament.

The passages in parentheses are interpreted as comments of the same type as verses 2:1-2, so they will be discussed in that connection.

Three of the four stanzas begin with the same phrase translated "If we go about saying," an effort to bring out the words as sayings or maxims characteristic of the pseudo-religion, perhaps a hodge-podge of Judaism and Gnosticism nearest to that in the Lycus Valley combatted by Paul's letter to the Colossians (2:8-3:4). The first two stanzas put false and true fellowship in contrast. *Koinōnia* (fellowship) with God is possible only in the light, for "God is light," so the false teachers who think they are in fellowship with God while they are walking about in moral darkness are living a lie. The lie belongs to darkness as truth belongs to light. The Greek word for truth *(alētheia)* means that which is no longer hidden. Moral integrity and intellectual integrity belong together as the marks of fellowship with God. The sinner and the liar are the same. Some live the lie and cover it up by telling the lie in the pious jargon which says: "We are having fellowship with God." Good religion is the best thing in the world, but false religion is the worst, for the highest possibility of all, fellowship with God, has become perverted.

Genuine religion is true fellowship with God, and this means to practice what we profess. It will be noted that most translations say "we are having fellowship with one another" rather than "with him," as in the above translation. The translation "with one another" has the strongest manuscript support, but it does not fit the context as well as the weaker reading which says "with him." Both are, of course, true in experience, but it is much easier to explain how later copies harmonized the passage with 1:3 than it is to explain how "with him" took the place of "with one another." The strongest support for "with him" is the same phrase in the first line of verse 6. Fellowship "with him" is the subject of both verses or stanzas, the first describing the false claim and the second the true fact.

Fellowship with God belongs to the heart of all true religion. Augustine was most certainly correct when he prayed for himself and man: "Thou has prompted him, that he should delight to praise thee, for thou hast made us for thyself and restless is our heart until it comes to rest in thee" (*Confessions* 1.1). The sure sign of false religion is the claim that fellowship with God can be maintained while living in sin.

The third and fourth stanzas are concerned with sin against God both in the present and in the past (1:8,10). If in the present we go about saying that we have no sin in our lives, it is disastrous in two ways. First of all, self-deception has taken place. It is easier to deceive ourselves than others, for we are unable to see ourselves as others see us until we accept ourselves as we really are. Sin has estranged us from God, and we do not see ourselves until we see ourselves as the sinners we are. One of the sickening things about self-deception is that it leads to the sophisticated assumption that others are as blind to our sins as we are, but this is never so.

The second disaster is the absence of truth in us. Truth lays things bare as they really are. It is the very opposite of deception that puts a mask on sin. It is the unmasking of sin that makes man free, and that is why knowing the truth is the way to freedom (John 8:32). The absence of truth is a characteristic of the devil. "He was a murderer from the beginning, and has nothing to do with the truth, because there is no truth in him" (John 8:44). Self-deception and the absence of truth are two sides of the same thing, for the absence of truth is self-deception.

The truth is brought out in the past tense (1:10). To say we have not sinned makes a liar of God who has dealt with us as sinners. The claim that we have never sinned is the refusal to see ourselves in the light of God's revelation of himself. God's revelation of himself is his word, so a rejection of his revelation as redeemer is a rejection of his word. Making God a liar and the absence of his word are again the two sides of the same truth.

Amos N. Wilder has well noted that there is an ascending order of seriousness in the false claims of this pseudo-religion: "we are having fellowship with him" (1:6); "we have no sin" (1:8); "we have not sinned" (1:10). These pseudo-sayings are countered with a corresponding charge that also ascends in seriousness: "we are lying and we are not doing the truth" (1:6); "we are deceiving ourselves and the truth is not in us" (1:8); "we are making a liar out of God and his word is not in us" (1:10).

The parenthetical comments are two. The first has to do with cleansing from sin. The means of this cleansing strikes at the heart of both Gnosticism and Judaism. Gnosticism denied the true humanity of Jesus, and cleansing from sin by blood would make their hair stand up in shock. Judaism denied that Jesus was the Son of God in the unique sense of Johannine theology, so that too is ruled out by this brief comment at the end of verse 7. It sounds one of the distinctive notes of the Letter, as comments on hymns often do.

The confession of sin picks up the idea of cleansing again (1:9). It will be noted that there are four lines in this verse. The first two make the confession of sin and the faithfulness of God corollaries. When man is honest with his sin, he may be sure that God will be just with him. The last two lines are also parallel, for the forgiveness of sin means very much the same as cleansing. Forgiveness means that sin is taken away, and cleansing means it is washed away. Sin and unrighteousness are also synonyms.

Fellowship with God and the forgiveness of sin are never separated in Christian experience. Cleansing from sin and the confession of sin are also inseparable, for God does not cleanse away sin in an objective way until there is the confession of sin in a subjective way.

(2) Sin and forgiveness (2:1-2).

> 1 My little children, these things I am writing to you that
>   you may not fall into sin;
>   and if any one does fall into sin
>   we have a Paraclete with the Father
>   Jesus Christ the Righteous One,

> 2 And he is the expiation concerning our sins,
>   and not concerning ours only
>   but also concerning the whole world's.

The Qumran *Manual of Discipline* has some powerful words about cleansing, but it is associated more with future judgment than with present fellowship (4:20-21). John shifts to the present. It is not until 2:3 that the "we" form returns, so the "I" form seems to be another parenthetical comment to state the purpose of the writing. Little children (*teknia*) is an address found seven times in the letter (2:1,12,28; 3:7,18; 4:4; 5:21), while young children (*paidia*) is found twice (2:14,18). *Teknia* focuses attention on the new birth and infancy, as *paidia* pertain to early education and childhood, but they are used of the same people and have very little difference in meaning in the present context. They seem to be synonyms in 2:12,14.

As the little children learn to walk, there is danger that they may fall into sin. Children of God do not continue to live in sin, as the present linear tense indicates (3:4-10), but they may fall into sin, and that is the meaning of the aorist (punctiliar) tense in 2:1. It is impossible to harmonize 1:7,9 and 2:1-2 unless this distinction in tenses is made. Sheep may fall into mud, but they do not live there; pigs may enjoy the warm sun on the hill, but they love the mud most. So it is with saints and sinners.

The Paraclete is Jesus Christ the Righteous One. The word Paraclete is used in the Gospel of John for the Holy Spirit (14:15-

17,25-26; 15:26-27; 16:4b-11,12-15).[1] This term has background in the Qumran writings.[2] In I John it has reference to Christ as he makes intercession for sinners as he appears before the Father in heaven, but in the Gospel of John it is "another Paraclete" (*allon parakleton*, 14:16) who represents Christ to the saints on earth. The difference is important, but there is really no contradiction. *Allon parakleton* means another of the same kind, not *heteron parakleton*, another of a different kind.

Jesus Christ as Paraclete is identified with the two main streams of thought in the Old Testament that prepared the way for the understanding of the death of Christ in the New Testament writings: the servant of the Lord and the sacrifice for sin. The suffering servant of Isaiah 53:11 was called the Righteous One, and Jewish Christianity identified Jesus with this Holy and Righteous One (Acts 3:14). This is perhaps the meaning when the Paraclete is called by this title (2:1). As Paraclete, Jesus Christ makes intercession for believers who fall into sin and need forgiveness. Christ as one who makes intercession for the priesthood of believers belongs to the high Christology of Hebrews (2:18; 4:14; 7:25; 9:24) and Paul (Romans 8:34) as well as the Johannine writings. The intercession of the Spirit and the intercession of Christ are found together in Paul (Romans 8:26,34).

Christ as sacrifice is more characteristic of the Johannine writings than the idea of the suffering servant, but it is not always clear what type of sacrifice is in mind. Here the sacrifice for sin seems to be behind the Greek word *hilasmos* (2:2). Much debate has gone on as to whether the right interpretation is that of propitiation (*Authorized Version*) or expiation (*Revised Standard Version*). There is no doubt that John has more than a subjective reconciliation to God in mind, but an objective view that goes so far as to say God must be placated or pacified before he will forgive sin is more pagan than Christian. The more biblical view of the verb, rarer in pagan writers, is that of an action that removes defilement. That is very near the meaning of forgiveness, and the previous comment said not only that "the blood of Jesus, His Son, makes

---

[1] Dale Moody, *Spirit of the Living God* (Philadelphia: The Westminster Press, 1968), pp. 164-175.

[2] Otto Betz, *Der Paraklet* (Leiden/Köln: E. J. Brill, 1963).

us clean from all sin" (1:7), but that a faithful and just God "will forgive our sins and cleanse us from all unrighteousness" (1:9). The word *hilasmos* is later used in 4:10 as the model for sacrificial love, and this hardly sounds like propitiation. It is John's use of the word that must first be considered, and it seems to be more in line with the biblical view of expiation.

The preposition used is *peri* (concerning), and this would hardly be expected with the idea of propitiation. The usual Pauline preposition is *hyper* (on behalf of another), and this may be called vicarious sacrifice, but the substitutionary preposition *anti* (in the place of another) is rare (I Timothy 2:6 where it is attached to the noun and followed by *hyper*). The idea of substitution is not to be excluded altogether, but the vicarious death of Jesus is distorted when it is put at the center.[3] The Johannine preposition *peri* is even more general than *hyper*, so the view of Christ as our representative before God agrees with the whole concept of Paraclete.

The penal substitutionary view of the death of Christ that says he died only for the elect (limited) is even more uncomfortable with this passage in I John. The sacrifice for sin is not limited to those with whom the writer identified himself. It is a sacrifice "concerning the whole world's." Sins must be supplied to the Greek, but there is little doubt that it is intended after each of the three times *peri* is used. It is possible, however, that the whole world is regarded as a mass of sin (5:19). In any case the sacrifice of Christ is not limited to "the elect." This is an agreement with the portrait of Jesus in the Gospel of John which proclaims: "Behold, the Lamb of God who takes away the sin of the world" (1:29. Cf. 3:16; 11:51-52). That is the meaning of "the world" in I John (2:15-17; 4:9,14; 5:4-5,19).

3. Keeping the commandments (2:3-11); obedience.

    (1) The commandments and knowledge (2:3-6).

      3 And by this we know that we have known him,
        if we keep his commandments.

---

[3] Leon Morris, *The Expository Times*, Vol. 62 (1951), pp. 227ff.; *The Cross in the New Testament* (Grand Rapids: Wm. B. Eerdmans Publishing Company, 1965), pp. 348-350. The criticisms of the propitiation view by T. C. G. Thorton seem valid, *The Expository Times*, Vol. 80 (1968), pp. 53-55.

4 Whoever goes about saying that "I have known him,"
    and does not keep his commandments
        is a liar and the truth is not in him;

5 but whoever keeps his word,
    truly in him love for God has been perfected.
    By this we know that we are in him.

6 (Whoever goes about saying he abides in him
    ought as that One walked
        also himself to walk).

Pirke Aboth, a Rabbinic tractate, says (4:13):

He who fulfills one commandment has gained for himself one
    paraclete;
he who commits one transgression has gained for himself one
    accuser.

The first line in the parallelism makes a definite connection between
the keeping of the commandments and a paraclete, but the differences are important. In I John 2:1 the paraclete is Jesus Christ,
and intercession is not gained by keeping the commandments.
He intercedes for the "little children" of God as an expression of
the love of God, as keeping the commandments expresses God's
love in the believer. The Rabbinic saying is based on merit, but
John's sayings are based on mercy.

Knowledge was the key concept of Gnosticism, as the word
indicates. The Gnostics sought to commend Christianity to the
Greek mind by making it a new and superior form of knowledge
(*gnōsis*). One pagan writer said: "This alone is salvation for a
man—knowledge of God" (*Corpus Hermeticum,* X.15). This is
very close to the words of Jesus, who said: "And this is eternal
life, that they know thee the only true God, and Jesus Christ
whom thou has sent" (John 17:3). The error of the Gnostics was
that they left out the mediation of knowledge through Jesus Christ
and taught an unmediated knowledge based on a mystical speculation without the incarnation.

This was also a mysticism without morality. Keeping the commandments of God was looked upon as belonging to those who
lived on the lower level. There was no hope for those who lived on

the level of flesh (*sarx*). Such were no better than animals. Those who lived on the level of soul (*psyche*) could rise up to the level of spirit and mystical knowledge by discipline of mind and body, but the perfect were not subject to moral commandments, so the Gnostics taught. I John 2:3 is then an outright rejection of this cleavage between the knowledge of God and the commandments of God. This seems to be the first parallel as the poetry is resumed.

The next three lines are a refutation of this pseudo-knowledge of God (2:4). It is again called pseudo because the teacher of this sophisticated and aristocratic claim to possess knowledge is a liar (*pseustēs,* cf. 1:8,10; John 8:44). It is a religion that used such catchwords (sayings, maxims) as "I have known him" when it was an outright lie. They were drowning in the sea of their own emotional egotism and knew neither God nor themselves. True knowledge and obedience to God belong together. The truth as it is in Jesus stands opposite to this lie, for the truth liberates man for God and his neighbor. Egotistic speculation is bondage to self.

True knowledge of God is obedience to God, and obedience to God is love for God. That is the logical connection between 2:4 and 2:5. Lines 2 and 3 in verse 4 state the negative side, while lines 1 and 2 in verse 5 state the positive side of knowledge as obedience and love. The above translation adopts the view of most translators and commentators that *agapē tou theou* means "love for God" and not "love of God" for man. It is possible to translate the phrase as a subjective genitive rather than as objective, but the use of the phrase in I John is against it (2:15; 3:17; 4:12; 5:3). The use in 4:12 is a close parallel, and the perfection of love is there clearly love for God (4:20-21). Love for God and keeping God's commandments are linked again in 5:3, so that seems to be the meaning in 2:5.

Love for God has often been discounted in the name of biblical thought. *Agape and Eros* by Anders Nygren, a great history of love, in some ways, has unfortunately promoted this disparagement. Both God's love for man and man's love for God are found in the *Dead Sea Scriptures.*[4] Love for God as the way for true knowledge of God is also taught in Paul. There is nothing

[4] J. C. O'Neill, *The Puzzle of I John.* (London: S.P.C.K., 1966), p. 15.

unworthy about this statement: "But if one loves God, one is known by him" (I Corinthians 8:3).

Perfect knowledge about which the Gnostics boasted begins with perfect love for God, and it will later be seen that perfect love for God includes love for our brothers in the fellowship, not that sophisticated attitude of superiority that creates an egotistic class of the elite. This type of teaching was used also by Paul to refute Gnostic tendencies (Colossians 1:28-29). Perverted perfectionism void of obedience and love has ever since been a threat to Christianity.

The same formula of "by this we know" is used to introduce a second step in the thought (2:6). Knowing God and abiding in God were closely related in Gnosticism. Indeed, it could have been called "Menism" (from *menein*, to abide or to remain), for it claimed to remain on the high level of knowledge (*gnōsis*). *Menein* is an important word in Johannine letters (2:6,10,14,17, 19,24,28; 3:6,9,14,15,17,24; 4:12,13,15,16; II John 2,9).

The pronouns "him" and "his" seem to have reference to God, but the "that One" is Jesus. (Cf. 3:3,5,7,16; 4:17; John 7:11; 9:12,28; 19:21 for the Johannine use of *ekeinos*, "that One"). Walking as Jesus walked is the sure sign that one abides in God. As Jesus made his abode in the light and love of God in the days of his flesh, so must his disciples who now profess to abide in God. Walking is a Hebrew metaphor for daily conduct that has already been introduced (1:7), but it is generally associated with the Pauline writings (Romans 13:13; Colossians 3:7; Ephesians 2:2, 10; 4:1,17; 5:2,8,15). Jesus was servant and sacrifice in 2:1-2, but he is now example or model for mystical communion with God. Mediation and mysticism are united in the incarnation, and both require obedience to the historical Jesus. One can never be a Christian with the intellect alone, for obedience and love require the commitment of the will to follow Jesus (cf. I Peter 2:21-25). Doctrines without deeds are dead.

(2) The new commandment and love (2:7-11).

> 7 Beloved, I am writing no new commandment to you,
>> but an old commandment which you had from the beginning;
>>> the old commandment is the word which you have heard.

8 Again, a new commandment I am writing to you which is true in
  him and in you,
      because the darkness is passing away,
          and the true light already shines.

9 Whoever goes about saying he is in the light
  and keeps on hating his brother
      is in the darkness (until now).

10 Whoever goes about loving his brother
   abides in the light,
       and in it there is no cause for stumbling.

11 But whoever goes about hating his brother
   is in the darkness
       and walks in the darkness (and he does not know where
       he is going, because the darkness has blinded his
       eyes).

The new commandment of love goes beyond the keeping of
God's commandments in general. The new commandment is based
on the newness that came with Jesus. Paul taught the same view
of history by using the contrasts between the two ages of the
present and the future that was inaugurated in Jesus (I Corinthians 1:28; 2:6) and the two covenants (II Corinthians 3:1-11;
Galatians 4:24). The metaphor of light returns to describe the difference made between the old and the new by the coming of light into
the darkness (2:7-8) and to express the difference between hate and
love by contrasting the light with the darkness (2:9-11). This is the
first of several times when Christians are called beloved (2:7;
3:2,21; 4:1,7,11; III John 1, 2, 5, 11).

Old and new (2:7-8). The commandment is old because the
believers have had it since conversion. This happened when they
first heard the gospel. It is old, also, in the sense that it is *eternal,*
for the phrase "from the beginning" always has some overtone of
eternity (1:1, 2:7,13,14,24; 3:11). The word for newness (*kainē*)
has reference to quality not to chronology and quantity. When
Jesus spoke of a new garment, he made a contrast between the
qualitatively new (*kainē*) and the old, but when he spoke of new
wine in contrast to the old, he used the word for the quantitatively
new (*neos*), since it was just more of the same (Luke 5:26-29).

The qualitative newness to the commandment of love came with the light that dawned in Jesus. The passing away of darkness with the dawning of the light is pronounced in John's Gospel: "I am the light of the world; he who follows me will not walk in darkness, but will have the light of life" (8:12). Light and love are linked together, for "God is light" and "God is love." Therefore, the newness of light is the newness of love: "A new commandment I am giving to you, that you love one another; even as I have loved you, that you also love one another" (John 13:34).

The words "which is true in him and in you" (not in Manuscripts 205, 397) are considered a parenthetical expression, but it is very difficult to determine whether the "him" is God or Jesus. I John 1:5 does not support the choice in *Today's English Version (Good News for Modern Man)*: "its truth is seen in Christ and also in you." It is true that the dawning of the true light came with Jesus. Wilder calls attention to the beautiful anticipation of this event in the *Testament of Levi* (18:3-4):

> Lighting up the light of knowledge as the sun the day . . .
> He shall shine forth as the sun on the earth, . . .
> And there shall be peace in all the earth.

Paul was also fond of this metaphor for the coming of Jesus (I Thessalonians 5:1-11; II Corinthians 4:1-6; Romans 13:11-14; Ephesians 5:14).

Hate and love (2:9-11). Hate is symbolized by darkness, so he who hates his brother lives in darkness. Hate is the will to destroy another person. It is the typical attitude of the godless *kosmos*, the world alienated from and hostile to God, toward the *koinōnia*, the fellowship or brotherhood of those reconciled to God and with one another (3:11). Hate is the mother of murder, for the will to destroy usually bears its fruit in action (3:15). He who professes to love God while he hates his brother is living a religious lie (4:20).

A brother in I John is more than one's fellowman. It is far worse to hate one who abides in light and love than to return hate for hate. Of course, the Christian is to love even those who hate him, but I John is thinking of the fellowship of light and love (2:9-11). The brethren are the children of God or the little

children (3:10-17). Love for a brother who is seen is love for God
who is not seen (4:20-21). It is impossible to express love for
God when one withholds love from a brother. Prayer for a brother
who has committed the mortal sin is not obligatory, but neither
is it forbidden (5:16). III John also used the term "brethren"
to indicate the brotherhood of Christians (3,5,10).

The hostile darkness, the habitation of hate, is that which is
outside the fellowship of light (1:5). Love does not live in the
dank darkness (2:8-11). As in creation, the light dispels the
darkness, and the darkness is unable to extinguish the light (John
1:5). Belief leads one out of darkness into the light, and the
believing life does not abide in darkness (John 12:35,46). It is
the either/or of the metaphors of darkness and light, of hate and
love, that drives one out of the nonsense of neutrality. As light
shines into darkness, one is forced to make a decision. This is the
crisis (krisis, judgment, John 3:19-21).

In the light there is no reason for one to stumble. The skandalon,
translated stumbling, is an Old Testament metaphor drawn from
the sharp native stone rising up through the earth to trip the
traveler. Jesus spoke of those who caused others to sin as putting
a stumbling stone in their way (Matthew 13:41; 16:23). The
Authorized (King James) Version interprets en autōi to mean "in
him," i.e., there is no cause for one to stumble over the one who
loves his brother, but the Revised Standard Version is perhaps
correct when it says "in it," i.e., there is no reason to stumble in
the light. The Today's English Version has followed the first view
and says "he has nothing in himself that will cause someone else
to sin." This may well be true, but the Revised Standard Version
fits the context better.

The next verse, which returns to the one who hates his brother,
supports the the idea of the location of the stumbling in the darkness, so the opposite would be true of the light (2:10). The one
who hates his brother lives in the darkness and walks in the
darkness, and that is why he is unable to avoid the stumbling stone
of sin. Walking in darkness is a metaphor for sin as well as hate
(1:6,7). It is also a metaphor for the lie that is lived in sin and
darkness, since it is the very opposite of the truth in which the
faithful walk (II John 4,6; III John 3,4). Darkness—hate—lie stand
over against light—love—truth.

The parenthetical statement is a comment on walking in darkness. He who walks in darkness "does not know where he is going, because the darkness has blinded his eyes." He, therefore, stumbles over the sharp stone and falls into sin. His blindness is one of hate, an idea condemned in late Judaism. J. C. O'Neill finds this praise of love and condemnation of hate in the *Testament of Gad* (3-7) and in the Qumran documents. One of the Qumran writings is *The War of the Sons of Light and the Sons of Darkness,* but the apocalyptic ideas of this writing are nearer to the Johannine Apocalypse (Revelation) than to the Johannine letters and especially the Gospel. This may suggest the chronological order of the writings. Realized eschatology increases as the apocalyptic hope recedes. Since the publication of C. H. Dodd's book on *The Parables of the Kingdom* (1935), the term "realized eschatology" has frequently been used to designate any system of eschatology that emphasizes the fulfillment of the promises of God at the first coming of Christ at the expense of a second coming of Christ in glory.

The idea of spiritual blindness finds full expression when Paul speaks of the Gentiles who walk "in the futility of their minds" and who "are darkened in their understanding, alienated from the life of God because of the ignorance that is in them, due to their hardness of heart" (Ephesians 4:17-18). As A. T. Robertson says: "In the Mammoth Cave of Kentucky the fish in Echo River have eye-sockets, but no eyes." The way is prepared for the Johannine teaching on the realm of darkness and light when Paul speaks of the conversion experience as a transfer from "the dominion of darkness" into "the kingdom of his beloved Son" (Colossians 1:13). Many of the readers of the Pauline writings were later the readers of the Johannine writings.

4. Overcoming the godless *kosmos* (2:12-17).

   (1) The blessings of the *koinōnia* (2:12-14).

   12 I am writing to you, little children,
   because your sins have been forgiven for his name's sake.

   13 I am writing to you, fathers,
   because you have known Him Who is from the beginning.

I am writing to you, young men,
>   because you have overcome the Evil One.

I wrote to you, young children,
>   because you have known the Father.

14 I wrote to you, fathers,
>   because you have known Him Who is from the beginning.

I wrote to you, young men,
>   because you are strong,
>   and the word of God abides in you,
>   and you have overcome the Evil One.

This beautiful passage bristles with problems of translation and interpretation, so alternate views will be reviewed. The literary questions may be noted first, since these are important for interpretation. With the exception of the last line, the above translation is a literal translation printed according to the pattern of *The Greek New Testament* now published by the United Bible Societies, the most scientific and accurate text available. The last line differs only on indentation!

The *Authorized (King James) Version* and the *Revised Standard Version* obscure the fact that the present tense ("I am writing") is used for the first three times and the past tense ("I wrote") for the last three. This is due to the view that the past tense may be the epistolary aorist, i.e., the past tense that is often used by a letter writer who speaks first from his point of view and then from the point of view of the reader. In a similar way, some say the present and the past tense are used simply for variety. J. C. O'Neill has suggested that the present tense is the viewpoint of the Christian editor and the past is that of the source which he is using. O'Neill should not be discounted simply because the view is new, for it is less strained than the other two views.

The theological questions have long intrigued expositors. The first question has to do with the three groups: little children or young children, fathers, and young men. In the Greek tradition of the Church Fathers, a spiritual interpretation of three stages in Christian knowledge was proposed by two of the greatest thinkers in the Ante-Nicene period. Irenaeus of Lyons (c. 130-c.

200), in his famous theory of recapitulation, saw at least three stages in what educational psychology today might call "the seven ages of man." His well-known words were: "He came to save all through himself; all, that is, who through him are born into God, infants, children, boys, young men and old. Therefore he passed through every stage of life: he was made an infant for infants, sanctifying infancy; a child among children, sanctifying those of this age, an example also to them of filial affection, righteousness and obedience; a young man amongst young men, an example to them, and sanctifying them to the Lord. So amongst the older men; that he might be a perfect master of all, not solely in regard to the revelation of the truth, but also in respect of each stage of life" (*Against Heresies*, II. xxii.4). Origen (c. 185-c. 254) applied these stages to progress in spiritual growth.

The Latin tradition was more literal. Augustine (354-430) sees these forms of address as ways to designate the blessings that come to each age group at once. C. H. Dodd adopts this view and appeals to a passage in the *Corpus Hermeticum* (XI.20) to justify the interpretation that the Christian mystic "has experience of all grades and stages at once." The passage says: "To be everywhere at once—in earth, in sea, in heaven; to be unborn, in the womb, young, old, dead, after death—this is to be fit for the knowledge of God." Some support for this view can be advanced by noting again that *teknia* ("little children") is often used as I John's form of address for all believers in Christ (2:1,12,28; 3:7,18; 4:4, 5:21). This is apparently true of the corresponding word *paidia* ("young children," 2:14,18; cf. John 21:5). Others are more literal than Augustine and Dodd and take the three forms of address in terms of physical age.

Many others, then, conclude that two special (fathers and young men) groups are addressed within the whole body of believers (little children or young children). This, however, hardly explains why certain blessings are singled out as appropriate for each form of address. It seems possible that the stages of spiritual growth taught by the Gnostics are being transformed in meaning by assigning to each some distinct view of Christ, and to this view attention is now given.

The three fundamentals of Christian faith in conflict with Gnostic speculation are perhaps (1) the forgiveness of sin, (2) the incarnation of the preexistent Christ, and (3) the victory of the gospel over the Evil One (Satan). The forgiveness of sin has already been noted in previous comments (1:7,9; 2:1-2). It appears again in the section that O'Neill has singled out as the editorial comment of a distinctively Christian type. When the past tense is used in what may be the source, it is the knowledge of the Father that is assigned to the "young children" (2:14). A Gnostic would certainly have less resistance to the fatherhood of God than to the forgiveness of sins for the sake of Jesus. His "name's sake" employs "the name" used hundreds of times in the Old Testament, but the "name" of Jesus is the basis for forgiveness in the mind of the writer (3:23; III John 7; John 1:12). This goes beyond both Judaism and Gnosticism. Forgiveness is the foundation of the Christian life, so it is associated with "little children." Knowledge of the Father is also appropriate for the "young children" who have come to know that the Father in heaven loves them (Cf. 1:2, 3; 2:1,15,16,22,23; 3:1; 4:14).

Knowledge of the preexistent One who became incarnate in Jesus is assigned to the fathers each time. O'Neill thinks the "that which was from the beginning" (the message, cf. 2:24), according to a variant reading in *Codex Vaticanus,* "should be adopted on the grounds that verse 14 would naturally be assimilated to verse 13 by careless scribes," but most manuscripts have "Him Who" *(ton,* not *to).* There seems to be no doubt that the pre-existence of Christ is taught in verse 13 (cf. 1:1, John 1:1). The fathers know the Son, and the "young children" know the Father in most texts! This again goes beyond both Judaism and Gnosticism or Gnostic Judaism.

The victory of the gospel over the Evil One is stated in both the present tense and the past tense passages (2:13-14). The perfect tense is used to express the victory, for the victory is permanent. The "young men" *(neaniskoi)* are described in such a way that one can hardly interpret the term in purely chronological terms. Physical growth and chronological age clarify the figurative meaning, but victorious Christian living seems to be the central concept. Forgiveness of sin and knowledge belong more to the beginning of the Christian life in the "little children" and the "young children" (infants, children), and knowledge of the eternal Son (or the eternal gospel) is the result of mature

Christian thought and living by the "fathers" of the faith, but victory over the Evil One describes the growing Christian in his increasing strength.

In Hellenistic towns the *neaniskoi* (young men) were those who qualified for training in the Gymnasia, a term still used in much European education for classical high education. Sobriety (*sōphrosynē*) was the guiding ideal, but victory in games was the goal. A model young man in mental, moral, and physical life has become in I John the pattern for progress in the Christian life. Infancy, childhood, and youth are stages in developing personality and are still accepted as important psychological and educational distinctions. It is a pity that many church members are still in the cradle roll when they should be well on toward graduation from the high school of victorious living. One paster pathetically remarked that a classification of the members of his church according to their spiritual growth would leave him with the largest cradle roll department in the Southern Baptist Convention.

The young men are strong because the word of God continues to abide in them. As a seed in soil grows toward fruition, so the abiding word matures the Christian life. As a lovely infant passes through all the normal stages of life to a ripe old age, so do the saints of God become mellow in the knowledge and fellowship of God. This is true whether "the word of God" is interpreted as the preexistent Son (1:1; John 1:1) or the message about God's victory in his Son (2:24; 3:11).

Victory over the Evil One is the victory of light over darkness, of Christ over the Devil (3:8,10). The Devil is the Greek for what the Hebrews called Satan, the liar and tempter of men (John 8:44; 13:2). He was the Ruler of this world (*kosmos*), defeated by the triumph of Christ in his death and resurrection (12:31). Jesus did not pray for his disciples to be taken out of this godless *kosmos*, but he did pray that they would be kept from the Evil One (John 17:15). I John teaches that the *kosmos* is still ruled by the Evil One, but the Evil One is unable to touch those who abide in the fellowship of light and love which was created by the coming of Christ into the world (5:18,19. Cf. John 10:27-29). It is the word of God abiding in the believer and the abiding of the believer in Christ that gives him victory over the Evil One. I John will later speak of those who abandon the fellowship (2:19,

5:16), but it is the victory of faith that is the emphasis here (cf. 5:4). There has been much effort exerted to "dedemonize" the New Testament, but the contrast between the Power of Darkness and the God of Light in I John puts one in the mood to pray again the prayer of our Lord: "Do not bring us to hard testing, but keep us safe from the Evil One" (Matthew 6:13, *Today's English Version*). As James Weldon Johnson put it on the lips of the good deacon in his prayer for the preacher: "Lord, keep him out of the gunshot of the Devil."

(2) The lusts of the godless *kosmos* (2:15-17).

15 Do not continue to love the godless world,
    neither the things that are in the godless world,
        If anyone continues to love the godless world,
            the love for the Father is not in him.

16 For all that is in the godless world
    (the lust of the flesh
        and the lust of the eyes
            and the vainglory of life)
    is not of the Father but of the godless world.

17   And the godless world is passing away and the lust of
            it,
                but he who goes on doing the will of God abides
                forever.

The word *kosmos* (world) is thus translated to emphasize its importance as that social organism estranged from God and hostile toward those who abide in the *koinōnia* of light and love. This grouping should not be dismissed as a vestige of Persian dualism that found fullest expression in Zoroastrianism and influenced Judaism from the time of the Babylonian Captivity. The idea of Ahura-Mazda, the god of light, does indeed color the Johannine view of God as light, as the idea of Angro-Mainyu, the power of darkness, contributed to the belief in Satan or the Devil, but that does not prove it wrong. The Power of Darkness, the Devil, is always a creature of God and never eternal in Scripture, but a temporal dualism between light and darkness is very real.

A word of exhortation comes first (2:15). Believers are called to stop loving or to cease loving the godless *kosmos*. This love is more of an attachment or an affection for the fallen *kosmos* than the *agape* that unites one to God and to his brother. The *kosmos* may at times be almost neutral in meaning, being the created world and those who live in it. It is used numerous times in most of the chapters in John's Gospel, and all shades of meanings may be found (cf. John 1:10; 3:16; 12:31; 17:24). In I John, however, the idea of a social system hostile toward God and his children seems to be present (2:2,15,17; 4:1,3,4,5,9,14,17; 5:4,5,19. Cf. II John 7). It is, therefore, impossible to love the godless *kosmos* that is hostile toward God and have love for the Father. Love for the godless *kosmos* and love for the Father exclude one another. Love for the Father is interpreted as an objective genitive as in "love for God" (2:5; 3:17; 4:12; 5:3). Love for God is again impossible without love for the Christian brother. The Father and the fellowship (*koinōnia*) belong together.

A world of elaboration describes the things that constitute the godless *kosmos* (2:16). The three phrases in parentheses advance the thought. The other two lines simply give the reason for the exhortation in 2:15. That which belongs to the godless *kosmos* does not belong to the Father. The temptations with which the serpent confronted Eve in the Garden of Paradise and those that Satan used on Jesus in the Wilderness Temptation parallel the summary of the godless *kosmos* in I John 2:16 (cf. Genesis 3:6; Matthew 4:1-11; Luke 4:1-13).

The lust (*epithumia*) of the flesh is more than sensuality. It includes sensuality to be sure, but the term includes all the desires growing out of a self-centered life that is hostile to God (cf. Galatians 5:16-21). The translation "the sensual body" in *The Jerusalem Bible* limits the concept too much. *Today's English Version* is just right when it says "what the sinful self desires." This was the food good to eat in Eden and the bread from stones in the Wilderness.

The lust of the eyes is superficiality of judgment interpreted in the literal sense of seeing things only on the surface. Wilder points out a passage in the *Testament of Reuben* (ch. 2) which speaks of a "sense of sight from which ariseth desire." Jesus warned against the lust in a look (Matthew 5:27-29). *Today's*

English Version is again superb with the translation of "what people see and want." Unscrupulous advertisement on paper and screen has unfortunately learned the way down this road to the human soul. This was that which was good to look upon in Eden and the kingdom of the world Satan showed to Jesus.

The vainglory (*alazoneia*) of life concerns the highest dimension of human personality. "Pride" is hardly strong enough. *Today's English Version* uses the paraphrase of "everything in this world that people are so very proud of," and this is almost necessary, but the one word "vainglory" is adequate. C. H. Dodd gives an abridged translation of a passage in Theophrastus' *Character's* (No. 23): "The *Alazon* is the kind of person who will stand on the mole and tell perfect strangers what a lot of money he has at sea, and discourse of his investments, how large they are, and what gains and losses he has made, and as he spins his yarns he will send his boy to the bank—his balance being a shilling. If he enjoys company on the road, he is apt to tell how he served with Alexander the Great, how he got on with him, and how many jewelled cups he brought home; and to discuss the Asiatic craftsmen, how much better they are than any in Europe—never having been away from Athens. He will say that he was granted a free permit for the export of timber, but took no advantage of it, to avoid gossip; and that during a corn shortage he spent more than fifteen hundred pounds in gifts to needy citizens. He will be living in a rented house, and will tell anyone who does not know the facts that this is the family residence, but he is going to sell it because it is too small for his entertainments." The *moron* is a fool because he has never grown up, but the *alazon* is a full-grown fool. He is, as Billy Sunday once said, all front door: when you go in, you are immediately in the backyard! He is a plain humbug.

A third word of explanation completes this classic summary on the world's lusts (2:17). The world is not only temporal; it is transitory; it is in the process of "passing away." It is as Robert Burns described pleasure in Tam O'Shanter:

> But pleasures are like poppies spread;
>   You seize the flow'r, its bloom is shed;
> Or like the snow falls in the river,
>   A moment white—then melts for ever;

God alone abides forever, so the world aliented from God is passing away and the lust of it. Man may abide forever in fellowship with God, but he perishes unless God's eternal life is imparted to him (John 3:16). God and that which is related to God abide, but all else is transitory. The words inscribed on the tomb of D. L. Moody were well chosen: "He who does the will of God abides forever." Therefore, "Moody still lives," as one biography is called, but so do all who left this world in fellowship with God.

> Change and decay in all around I see;
> O thou, who changest not, abide with me.

5. Guarding against the enemy (2:18-27): antichrists.

(1) The antichrists are those who depart from the *koinōnia* (2:18-21).

18 Young children, it is a last hour,
    and just as you have heard that an Antichrist is coming,
        so now many antichrists have come;
            therefore, we know that it is the last hour.

19 They went out from us, because they were not of us;
    for if they had been of us, they would have continued
        with us;
            but they went out that it might be manifested that
            all are not of us.

20 (But you have a *chrisma* from the Holy One, and you know all things).

21 I wrote not to you because you do not know the truth,
    but because you know it,
        and that no lie is of the truth.

The discussion up to this point has the background of light and the general topic of soteriology—the study of the plan and purpose of salvation. Future eschatology is now interpreted in the light of the promise of Eternal Life. After the exhortations about the age of the antichrists (2:18-27), the future manifestation of God at the *parousia* (2:28-3:3) and the past manifestation of Christ as the preparation for the *parousia* (3:2-10) will be interpreted in the light of the inauguated eschatology already noted (2:8). (The Greek word *parousia* generally means the second coming of Christ, and it is rapidly becoming an English word in much the same manner as *koinōnia*—fellowship.)

The address of "young children" (*paidia*) has also appeared already (2:14), but it will soon yield again to such terms as little children (*teknia*, 2:28; 3:7,18; 4:4; 5:21) and "beloved" (*agapētoi*, 3:2,21; 4:1,7,11). *Paidia* each time is related to the learning process as *teknia* has to do with the new birth and *agapētoi* with the new brotherhood.

Time is an important topic in biblical teachings. The Old Testament speaks first of the last days as the time just before entrance into the Promised Land (Genesis 49:1), and this became the model for the good times in store for the faithful (Isaiah 2:2). Disobedience to the covenant relationship may, however, make the last days a period of bad times called the Day of the Lord (Amos 5:18-20). These days of woe would indeed be followed by days of weal, so out of this twofold expectation of doom and hope arose the time concept of the two ages, the present evil age which would end in a great tribulation and the coming age of glory which would be the age of the ages.

The New Testament adopted the concept of the two ages (Matthew 12:31; I Corinthians 2:6; Galatians 1:4). Such variations as "the last time" (Jude 18), "later times" (I Timothy 4:1), "last days" (II Timothy 3:1), and "the age of the ages" (Revelation 20:10; 22:5) are also found. The general idea is that of a crisis in which one age comes to an end and a new age begins. This biblical time line of history has often been dismissed by those who would reduce eschatology to a moment of decision so that every day is the last day, every hour is the last hour, and every moment the last moment. The moment of decision is important, but biblical eschatology is too stubborn to submit to this existential reduction.

The Johannine teachings on the meaning of a certain day or a certain hour are far more than existential decision. Seven times the Gospel of John speaks of "the last day," usually as the time of resurrection (6:39,40,44,54; 7:37; 11:24; 12:48), and the exception has reference to the last day of the feast of tabernacles (7:37). Seven times the "glorification" of Jesus by his own death and resurrection is called "my hour" (2:4; 7:30; 8:20; 12:23,27; 13:1; 17:1). The idea of the present *krisis* (crisis, judgment, 3:19) is very important also for the present decision men must make, but the past event of the death and resurrection of Jesus remains as a real event at the center of history as the resurrection of the dead remains a real event at the end of history. Decision in the present does not dispel the two comings of the Christ even in "the spiritual" Gospel of John.

The concept of the two comings of the Christ are the goal posts of the age of antichrists in I John. The Christ will come at the *parousia* (2:28-3:3) as surely as he has come at the passion (3:4-10), and the appearance of the antichrists at the present are the forerunners of the Antichrist who will come just before the *parousia* of the Christ. Some commentators seem to think I John displaces the future Antichrist with the concept of present antichrists, but this has no support in the text. The view of a future Antichrist is accepted as the belief in many present antichrists is argued.

The word Antichrist is found in Scripture only in the Letters of John (2:18,22; 4:3, II John 7), but the idea is old. The idea of enemies or of one supreme Enemy of God dwelling in the Desert, the Deep, the Darkness, or some other inhuman place is as old as religion itself. In the Old Testament the LORD does battle with the Dragon, Leviathan, and Rahab in creation (Isaiah 27:1; 51:9; Psalm 89:10; Job 26:13).

God's Adversary becomes historized as man's Enemy in biblical apocalypses. In the apocalypse of Daniel, Antiochus Epiphanes is viewed as the embodiment of evil and called the Abomination of Desolation (9:27; 11:31; 12:11). The Synoptic Apocalypse, at times called "the Little Apocalypse," adopts the term Abomination of Desolation to express the monstrous evil manifested in a figure like the Emperor Caligula and puts it in a three act drama of sufferings, tribulation, and the end (Mark 13:14). The Pauline Apocalypse, which may be called "the Tiny Apocalypse," speaks of the Man of Lawlessness who will be destroyed by Christ in a seven act drama (II Thessalonians 2:1-12). A Johannine Apocalypse is a panorama of events related to the revelation of Jesus Christ in glory after the destruction of the Beast, a monstrous figure who gathers qualities of previous images into a personality like unto

Nero and Domitian (Revelation 13:1,11; 16:13; 17:3,7,7-12; 19:20; 20:10).[5]

The concept of many antichrists who precede the Antichrist is not novel. It is another way to describe the false prophets in other apocalyptic passages (Mark 13:21-22; Matthew 24:1-12,23-24; Luke 21:8). In the Old Testament the false prophets were interpreted as instruments of a "lying spirit" (I Kings 22:15-23), and this view is expressed in I John (4:6). The many antichrists were the Gnostic heretics who denied that Jesus Christ had come in the flesh (4:1-6).

The heresy of the Gnostics soon led to schism (2:19). There is a play upon the double meaning of the preposition *ek* (out of, from) in the statement: "They went *ex hēmōn* because they were not *ex hēmōn*." A. T. Robertson points out John 17:14-15 as an example of *ex* in the sense of likeness along with *ex* in the sense of origin and translates the first *ex hēmōn* as "from us" and the second as "of us," a view adopted by all translators. "They had lost the inner fellowship and then apparently voluntarily broke the outward." The statement is often quoted as if it says "they *never were of us*" (JB, NEB), but Robertson reads the statement more carefully. They were perhaps at one time a part of the fellowship, but the heresy they embraced broke this fellowship and led to schism. Their departure made manifest the breach of inner fellowship. Heresy was more dangerous for the fellowship than a brother who committed mortal sin, but both were creating a crisis in Asia.

The threat of this Gnostic heresy and schism continued to the end of the second century. At the beginning of the century Ignatius of Antioch (c. 35-c. 107) said of the same heresy: "Flee, then, these wicked offshoots which produce deadly fruit. If a man taste of it, he dies outright. They are none of the Father's planting. For had they been, they would have shown themselves as branches of the cross, and borne immortal fruit" (*Trallians* 11:1-2). Irenaeus of Lyons (c.130-c.200), who was reared in Asia, associated the heresy with a leader named Cerinthus who said that Christ descended on Jesus only at his baptism but flew back to the Father before Jesus died on the cross (*Against Heresies*, I.xxvi.1). Irenaeus

---

[5] For more details see Dale Moody, *The Hope of Glory* (Grand Rapids, Michigan: Wm. B. Eerdmans Publishing Company, 1964), ch. 7.

also looked upon the heresy as a form of Gnostic Judaism (I.xxvi.2).

The statement about an anointment (*chrisma*) from the Holy One is perhaps a comment which anticipates the fuller statement later (2:22,27). The uncertainty of its meaning may be seen by comparing the translations in the *New English Bible* and *Today's English Version*. The first, following the view of C. H. Dodd, says: "You, no less than they, are among the initiated; this is the gift of the Holy One, and by it you all have knowledge." The second says: "But you have had the Holy Spirit poured out on you by Christ, so all of you know the truth." The translations differ on two of the three problems confronted.

The first question is the meaning of the Greek noun *chrisma* which has been left untranslated above. C. H. Dodd challenges the traditional view by appealing to a practice in the mystery religions. The negative side appears in a letter to the Ephesians by Ignatius of Antioch in which he warns against being "anointed with the foul smell of the teaching of the prince of this world" (17:1). Hippolytus of Rome quotes the positive view in which the Gnostics say: "We alone of all men are Christians, who complete the mystery at the third portal and are anointed there with speechless chrism" (*Philosophoumena*, V.9. 121-2). The strongest support for this view in I John are the statements about the *chrisma* being "received" and "taught" and that it "teaches" (2:27). If Dodd is correct, the *chrisma* would be the apostolic doctrine.

It seems more likely that the *chrisma* is an Old Testament idea that has been developed in the New Testament and that the practice in the mystery religions perverted the practice in the apostolic age. Saul as a king, Elisha as a prophet, and Aaron and his sons as priests were anointed with oil as a sign of their role in the covenant relationship (I Samuel 9:16; 10:1; Exodus 29:7; I Kings 19:16). This became the practice in ancient Israel (cf. Samuel 16:3,12; I Kings 19:15-16; Leviticus 16:32). The prophetic proclamation in Isaiah 61:1, in which the LORD anointed the prophet to bring good news, was read by Jesus and applied to himself in the synagogue at Nazareth (Luke 4:16-20). Jesus is called the Christ (the Anointed) because God anointed him with the Spirit (Acts 10:38). That is why the baptism of Jesus is so significant in the Synoptic Gospels.

The anointment of a Christian is mentioned in the same context as the sealing in II Corinthians 1:22, and many commentators believe the anointment with the Spirit was associated with the baptismal "sealing" (cf. Ephesians 1:13; 4:30). G. W. H. Lampe has shown that this was the theology of baptism and confirmation in the Church Fathers and that the Gnostic practice of anointing was suspect.[6] This would give the *chrisma* much the same meaning as the Paraclete in the Gospel of John (14:15-17, 25-26; 15:26-27; 16:4b-15).[7] With this background and context in Scripture, George Johnston may be right in calling Dodd's view that has made its way into the *New English Bible* a thing "far fetched," and for these reasons the interpretation in *Today's English Version* is accepted.

The second question is the meaning of the Holy One. *Today's English Version* says Christ is the Holy One, but this is doubtful (but see John 6:69; Revelation 3:7). It is true that the Paraclete is said to be sent by Jesus (John 15:26; 16:7), but the Father gives and the Spirit proceeds from the Father (14:16; 15:26). Echoes of Isaiah 53:10-11 have already been heard (2:1-2), and it is not improbable that the term Holy One, found twenty-eight times in Isaiah, has been drawn from that source (cf. John 17:11). As God anointed Jesus with the Holy Spirit, so now, as the Holy One, he anoints all who confess Jesus to be the Son of God.

The third question is a textual problem. Both the *New English Bible* and *Today's English Version* have followed the reading of *pantes* (all) in *Codex Sinaiticus* and *Codex Vaticanus* and given the meaning which refutes the Gnostic claim that only the elite have a secret knowledge of deeper truth. The idea that such knowledge is open to all was taught by Paul as he wrote to Christians in the same area as those addressed in I John (Colossians 1:28), and the manuscript support is strong indeed, but the reading is far from certain. J. C. O'Neill points out that *oidate* (you know) never appears without an object as the reading of *pantes* (all) requires. The reading of *panta* (all things), found in *Codex Alexandrinus,* etc., is the object of *oidate* (cf. 2:21), and a number of able scholars prefer this reading. A close parallel in thought is found in one of the Paraclete sayings: "He will guide

---

[6] *The Seal of the Spirit* (London: Longmans, Green and Co., 1951).
[7] Dale Moody, *Spirit of the Living God,* pp. 164-181.

you into all truth" (John 16:13, cf. 16:15). This second view has been followed in the above translation (cf. *Authorized (King James) Version*).

The meaning is much the same in the two readings, as the next verse makes plain (2:21). In both, the Gnostic claim is rejected. The recipients of I John already possess the truth of the letter, so they need only to be reminded of the apostolic truth. Approaches of this type were made by Paul (I Thessalonians 4:9; I Corinthians 1:5), especially to the Roman Christians in a church he had not founded (1:12; 15:14-15), but the conception of truth that is available to all has special significance in the refutation of the Gnostic elite. Knowledge of the apostolic truth is the best defense against heresy, then and now.

(2) The antichrists are those who deny that Jesus is the Christ (2:22-25).

22 Who is the liar but he who denies that Jesus is the Christ?
    This is the Antichrist, he who denies the Father and the Son.

23 Everyone who denies the Son does not have the Father,
    whoever confesses the Son has the Father also.

24 Let what you heard from the beginning abide in you.
    If what you heard from the beginning abides in you,
        than you will abide in the Son and in the Father.

25 (And this is what he promised us, eternal life).

The lie of 2:21 is the link word for the liar of 2:22 (cf. 1:6,10; 2:4,21). The second heresy of Gnostic Judaism now comes up for refutation. Up to this point the humanity of Jesus has been the thumping point on the Gnostic heads (1:1-4,7,9; 2:1-2). Now the deity of Jesus as the incarnation of the Christ is defended against the Gnostic claim that one can have God the Father without Jesus the Son. The first four lines are concerned with confessing the Son at the beginning of the Christian life (2:22-23), and the next three are about abiding in the Son in the continuation of Christian living (2:24). The last line is a comment central for the whole section (2:25, cf. 2:18-3:10).

The concept of confession is central at all levels of New Testament faith. Confession and denial were decisive for the disciples of Jesus (Mark 8:28; Matthew 10:32-33; Luke 12:8-9). The confession in the margin of the *Revised Standard Version* at Acts 8:27 illustrates the connection between confession and Christian baptism, and the pledge (*eperōtēma*) of I Peter 3:21 indicates its place in the baptismal service. Confession is a major concept in the Hellenistic Jewish Christianity of Hebrews (4:14; 10:23; 13:15). The great confession of "Jesus is Lord" runs through the Pauline letters like a refrain (I Corinthians 12:3; Romans 10:9-10; Philippians 2:11), and the first reference illustrates the very opposite of false prophecy. As the confession of Jesus as Lord is inspired by the Holy Spirit, so the denial is inspired by the Devil (cf. 4:1-6).

The content of confession in I John 2:22-23 was impossible for the Gnostics. Their denial of Jesus as the Christ was blasted as a lie, because the fellowship confessed it as the truth. The antichrist is the liar because he denies the truth as it is in Jesus. They were able to confess a Christ who was an aeon between God and man, but they were unable to say that the Christ was a man (4:2). This Gnostic idea pops up at the present among those who divide "the Christ idea" from the "Jesus of history." The Christ alone preexisted, but in the incarnation Jesus and Christ are one, but Gnosticism could do no better than adoptionism between baptism and the cross.

The Jesus-Christ relation turns toward the Father-Son relation. Some of the Gnostics could talk of a First Father who is "absolute Being, eternal Reason, or the Unfathomable Depth," as Dodd points out, but they were unable to believe in God as Father of Jesus Christ, his Son. Fatherhood—yes, but Sonship—no, they argued. Johannine faith was based upon the belief that the two are unseparable. The full revelation of the Father is in the Son (John 1:18; 14:6-9. Cf. Matthew 11:27; Luke 10:22). The relationship between the Father and the Son must not be broken (cf. John 5:23; 10:30, 12:44-45; 15:23). Therefore, the faith that overcomes the world is summarized in the confession that "Jesus is the Son of God" (I John 5:5).

Abiding in this doctrine is abiding in the Father and the Son (2:24). It is in style now to separate abiding in a doctrine from abiding in a person, much as the "Christ idea" is separated from the "historical Jesus," but Johannine theology would classify this as a new form of Gnosticism, as indeed it is. The two must be kept together. "Any one who goes ahead and does not abide in the doctrine of Christ does not have God; he who abides in the doctrine has both the Father and the Son" (II John 9). This is the eternal message, that which "you heard from the beginning" (cf. 2:7). "Do not be carried away by the new-fangled Gnostic teaching" (A. T. Robertson).

It is, of course, possible to hold to the doctrine of the incarnation in such a wooden way that it gives no evidence of mystical union with the Father and the Son. That type of orthodoxy has often turned as many away from Christ as heresy, but neither is the mystical "menism" of John. Menism is a term coined from the Greek *menein*, to abide. It is used to avoid some of the pagan implications of the term mysticism. Menism emphasizes the eternal distinction between God and man and the role of Christ in the mediation of eternal life to man. John's mysticism is Christian, and one does not abide in God who does not abide in Christ. Abiding in Christ is eating the bread of heaven daily and bringing forth fruit like branches in a vine (John 6:22-71; 15:1-10). It is abiding in the light, life and love of God (2:10,25; 4:16).

The comment about God's promise of eternal life is one of the great declarations in I John (1:5; 2:25; 3:11,23; 4:3,21; 5:3,4,6,9, 11,14,20). This one modifies the basic teachings not only on the Antichrist but on future manifestation of God and past manifestation of Christ (3:4-10). The promise of eternal life makes all theology a theology of hope. Eternal life is nothing less than God's life imparted to those who abide in Christ (5:11,12).

(3) The antichrists are those who would deceive the anointed (2:26-27).

26 (These things I wrote to you concerning those who would deceive you.)

27 And as for you the *chrisma* which you received abides in you, and you have no need that any should teach you;

> but his *chrisma* teaches you concerning all things,
> and is true and is not a lie.
>> (And just as it taught you, abide in him.)

The antichrists would deceive those who are faithful even after their departure from the fellowship of those whose doctrine they denied. The apostolic witness now reduced to writing is obviously needed or the Letter would not exist. The early church soon realized that the internal testimony alone would lead to theological fantasies that were a contradiction to the great fundamentals. Scripture alone has led to a dead orthodoxy, but Spirit alone has produced fanaticism as some "spiritual" Anabaptists and Quakers later proved. As Jesus and Christ and the Father and the Son must be kept in focus, so must Scripture and Spirit.

That the *chrisma* is the Holy Spirit has already been discussed (2:22), but it is now expanded (2:27). The first two lines would lead to misguided enthusiasm if they were detached from the last two. The *chrisma*, the anointment with the Holy Spirit, is first teacher. This is a clear parallel with the second saying about the Paraclete (John 14:25-26). In the second place, the *chrisma* is truth. This means its teaching is in harmony with the apostolic truth and a refutation of the Gnostic lie. This has a parallel in the fifth Paraclete saying (John 16:12-15). Here again "all things" is the object as in the above translation of 2:20. The text of *Codex Vaticanus*, which omits *hōs* (as), has been followed.

The last line could be translated with "just as he taught," if the human teacher is in mind, but "it taught" makes it a reference to the *chrisma*, the Holy Spirit. Both are true, but it seems to be a comment about the *chrisma*. The two statements in parentheses form a balance between the external witness of Scripture and internal witness of the Holy Spirit. The anointment and the abiding are now brought together in preparation for the exhortations about the *parousia*. The "him" seems to be God the Father who is light. Fellowship with him (1:6-10), knowing him (2:3-6), and abiding in him (2:27) seem to be God in this first division, even though the Son is twice included (1:3; 2:24). Abiding in God is abiding in the light (2:10). The distinction between "him" and "that One" who is Jesus has already been noted (2:6; cf. 3:3). This is a God-mysticism mediated through Christ.

Chapter 4

COMMENTARY ON THE FIRST LETTER OF JOHN

LIFE (2:28-4:6)

1. Avoiding sin (2:28-3:10a).

(1) The preparation of God's children for the *parousia* (2:28-3:1).

28 And now, little children, abide in him,
> so that when he is manifested we may have confidence
>> (*parrēsia*)
> and not shrink from him in shame at his coming
>> (*parousia*).

29 If you know that he is righteous,
> you know that everyone who does righteousness
>> has been begotten by him.

3:1 See what manner of love the Father has given to us,
> that we should be called children of God (and so we are).
> Therefore the godless world does not know us,
>> because it did not know him.

The arrangement of the Greek text into four couplets by J. C. O'Neill has been followed in the above translation, and some of his suggestions have been very valuable for interpretation. The most crucial question is the meaning of "him," "he," and "his." Do these have reference to God or to Jesus? All commentators and translators agree that "begotton by him" must mean the same as "begotten by God" (3:9), but a mixture of interpretations is found on the rest. The following interpretation assumes that in every instance the pronoun has reference to God (cf. 2:3-6,20,27). This seems the only way to avoid the inconsistency of the more traditional interpretations and translations.

The observation of *The Jerusalem Bible* that the general topics of the first part (1:5-2:27) are reviewed again from a new perspective is also helpful, although the details of the following outline differ. There is first of all a section on avoiding sin (2:28-3:10a), and this is followed by sections on keeping the commandments (3:10b-24) and guarding against the antichrists in the godless *kosmos* (4:1-6). The section on avoiding sin has three clearly marked parts of four couplets each with two couplets of comments in the second part (3:5-6) and one in the third (3:8b). The three parts instruct God's children on how to live in the *koinōnia* until the unredeemed *kosmos* comes to an end at the *parousia*. The three Greek nouns in the previous sentence are almost too distinctive to translate with English words, so they are adopted into the English language much as baptism has been.

The preparation of God's children for the manifestation of God at the *parousia* has a play on two Greek nouns in the first couplet (2:28). *Parrēsia* (confidence, boldness) is used in I John four times, twice in reference to the *parousia* (2:28; 4:17) and twice in reference to prayer (3:21; 5:14). It means "freedom of speech" before God whether at the final judgment or in prayer at the present.[1]

The second word is *parousia,* the manifestation of God in glory at the final judgment. In the New Testament the word is usually used of Jesus Christ as he returns at the second coming, but it is also used of human beings (I Corinthians 16:17; II Corinthians 7:6,7; 10:10; Philippians 1:26; 2:12) and of the Man of Lawlessness (II Thessalonians 2:9). This is the only time it appears in the

---

[1] W. C. Van Unnik, *The Christian's Freedom of Speech in the New Testament* (Manchester: John Rylands Library, 1962), pp. 485-486.

Johannine writings and the only time in the New Testament that it is used of God, but there are parallels in Jewish documents. A striking parallel is found in the *Testament of Judah* (22:2):

> And among men of another race shall my kingdom be brought
> to an end,
> > until the coming of the salvation of Israel,
> > > until the *parousia* of the God of righteousness.

The Day of Judgment passed through a parallel development from Day of the LORD to the Day of the Son of Man to the Day of Jesus Christ.[2]

The God of righteousness has already been mentioned in I John (1:9), although the word is used of Jesus (2:1), but to say "Christ is righteous," as in *Today's English Version*, is to bring it into conflict with "begotten of him" (2:20). If "he" and "him" do not have the same reference, it is indeed true that, as J. C. O'Neill says, "the author must have had a bad lapse of concentration to have passed from the Son to the Father without noticing what he had done." A. T. Robertson, the great grammarian, can do no better than to say that *ex autou* (of him) apparently means "of God" and that "in spite of *dikaios* referring to Christ." The couplet is consistent only if both "he" and "him" refer to God. The righteous God begets his own righteous children. In the vocabulary of Paul, Jesus is the eternal Son, but God is said to adopt his son, a Christian (Galatians 4:4-6), but John never calls Christians sons of God. Christ alone is called Son in the Johannine writings, and Christians are begotten children (2:29; 3:9; 4:7; 5:1,14,18). The use of "sons of God" (John 1:12) and "only begotten" of the Son (John 3:16) in the *Authorized (King James) Version* are errors of translation.[3] Hellenistic mysticism made regeneration a human achievement rather than an act of God, and it is this against which John writes. The third century *Corpus Hermeticum* (X31.2-3) has preserved the Gnostic teachings on regeneration.

God bestows his love on the children he has begotten. This is the manner of his amazing love. Here again, God is Father ("the Father" expresses the Johannine teaching of love, cf. 2:1 with

---

[2] Moody, *The Hope of Glory*, ch. 8.
[3] For details see Dale Moody, "Only begotten," in *The Interpreter's Dictionary of the Bible*.

references). In the Old Testament a name is of great significance, and the importance of a name is behind this exclamation about God making it possible for believers to be called his begotten children (*tekna*). *Teknia* (little children) is often used (2:1 with references), but *tekna* also carries the idea of tender love. Jesus himself taught that one of the blessings of peacemakers would be their designation, perhaps in the future, as "sons of God" (Matthew 5:9), but here the begotten are called children of God even in the present. This is not acknowledged by the unredeemed *kosmos*, for only those who know God know his children (3:1), as those who love God love his children (5:2). This same explanation is given the world's hatred of Jesus and his disciples (John 15:18-19), but here it is God and his children. The "and so we are" (*kai esmen*) is missing in some manuscripts, but it may be a typical Johannine parenthesis which anticipates the *esmen* (we are) of the next verse (3:2. Cf. John 5:25; Revelation 3:9).

(2) The purification of God's children before the *parousia* (3:2-6).

2 Beloved, now we are God's children;
    and it is not yet manifested what we shall be,

    but we know that if it is manifested we shall be like him,
    for we shall see him as he is.

3 And everyone who has this hope based on him
    purifies himself as that One is pure.

4 Everyone who does sin does also lawlessness,
    for sin is lawlessness.

5 (And you know that that One was manifested that he might bear sins,
        and in him there is no sin.

6 And everyone who abides in him does not practice sin;
    everyone who continues to sin has neither seen him nor known him.)

Here the Hebrew and the Hellenistic views on the Vision of God collide. Gnosticism taught that mystical contemplation could lead to a direct Vision of God here and now in human history, but the dominant Hebrew view was that sinful man could not look upon the LORD, the Holy One of Israel, and live. Direct Vision of God awaits the perfection of man. Jesus taught that the pure in heart would see God in the future, but not in the present (Matthew 5:8). Hellenistic Jewish Christianity believed the Radiance of God's glory appeared in Jesus Christ the Son of God, but direct Vision of God awaited at the end of the highway of holiness (Hebrews 1:13; 12:14). Pauline theology called Jesus the Image of God, and the glory of God shined in his face, but direct Vision is beyond this present evil world (I Corinthians 13:12; II Corinthians 3:18; Romans 5:2; 8:19,29; Colossians 3:1-4). Johannine Christianity remained faithful to this Hebrew heritage (John 1:14,18; 12:45; 14:9,19,21; 17:27). The nearest thing to a present Vision of God by the disciples of Jesus is the mystical manifestation called an *Emphany* (John 14:21f), but this is not to the world. The claim that this direct Vision of God is granted for brief periods to some elite souls was disputed in the Middle Ages. Even Thomas Aquinas believed it was possible under exceptional circumstances, as in the case of Moses and Paul (Exodus 34:25-28; II Corinthians 12:2-4).

This question is in the background of I John 3:2-6. Three steps are noted: (1) the future manifestation of God's children in God's likeness (3:2) is based upon (2) the present process of their purification (3:3-4) and (3) the past manifestation of the Son of God to bear away sins (3:5-6). It will be noted that manifestation has reference to God's children in both couplets (3:2) and not to God, as in 2:28, and not to Christ, as in 3:5-6. It is the second couplet that is possible to translate "he" rather than "it," but A. T. Robertson decided in favor of "it" as in the above translation. God's children will be like God when they see him, but at present they are only in the process of purification and transformation.

The present process of purification is motivated by the hope that is based on God (3:3). Without God no likeness to God is possible! This process of purification is the same as the process of cleansing by the blood of Jesus Christ (1:7,9), but self-purification is the human side of the process. The "that One" is later interpreted as

Jesus (3:5-6), and that seems always the meaning in Johannine theology (2:6; 3:5,7,16; 4:17; John 7:11; 9:12,28; 19:21).

Sin is defined as lawlessness, and is the very opposite of righteousness (2:29; 3:7-8). Sin is a process or practice as purification is a process. The translation of "does" for the present participle and the present indicative is an effort to put the process of sin over against the process of purification (3:3-4). Purification was practiced by the Jews at the Passover (John 11:55), and this is the lesson to be learned when Jesus washed the disciples' feet (John 13:1-11). After the bath of regeneration it is necessary for the disciples to wash away each sin: "He who has bathed does not need to wash, except for his feet, but he is clean all over; and you are clean, but not all of you" (John 13:10).

The past manifestation of God's Son as Jesus Christ was to bear away sins (3:5-6). Here "that One" is clearly Jesus (cf. 2:6; 3:7,16; 4:17). His manifestation was the incarnation (1:2). As such, he was "the Lamb of God who takes away the sin of the world" (John 1:29). The couplet has "sins" in the first line and "sin" in the second, but the verb is the same as in John 1:29. Already the influence of the Old Testament teaching on the servant of the LORD and the sacrifice for sin has been noted, and the Day of Atonement and perhaps the Passover (cf. Hebrews 10:4,11). The absence of sin in him in the days of his flesh (John 7:18; 8:46; Hebrews 4:15) and in his sacrifice (Hebrews 7:26; 9:13) is now applied to abiding in him. Here "him" applies to the Son of God who took away sin, for "fellowship is with the Father and with his Son Jesus Christ." The translation of "practice sin" (present active) and "continues to sin" (present participle) again attempts to bring out the continuous action. There is no sin in God's Son as there is no darkness in God (1:5).

J. C. O'Neill is perhaps correct in seeing this as a comment in addition to the second group of four couplets, but the reference to "that One" (3:3) does not support the idea that the original hymn belonged to the Jewish community of faith. This is the fourth comment concerned with cleansing from sin (1:7b,9; 2:1-2; 3:5-6). These are all anti-Gnostic.

(3) The manifestation of God's children before the *parousia* (3:7-10a).

7 Little children, let no one deceive you.
  Whoever does righteousness is righteous
      just as that One is righteous.

8 Whoever continues to sin is of the Devil;
      for the Devil has sinned from the beginning.

  (For this reason the Son of God was manifested
      in order that he might destroy the works of the Devil).

9 Everyone who is begotten of God does not make a practice of
  sin
      because his seed abides in him;

  and he is not able to make a practice of sin
      because he has been begotten of God.

10 (By this is manifested the children of God
      and the children of the Devil).

For the fourth time the readers are addressed as little children (2:1,12,28; 3:7,18; 4:4; 5:21). The danger of deception is sounded again (2:26; 3:7. Cf. 1:8), and this section on avoiding sin again has four couplets. Each pair of couplets is followed by a comment. The first two couplets speak of the behavior of God's children (3:7-8), and the second two explain their behavior by speaking of their being begotten of God (3:9).

Their behavior is a matter of what they are. A righteous person is one who does righteousness. One is what he does, and the model for what he does is Jesus. Jesus is that One who is the example of Christian conduct (2:3), who is holy, (3:3) and who was manifested to bear sins (3:5). There is no conflict between Jesus the example and Jesus the sacrifice for sin, and any effort to pull them apart is a distortion of the gospel. Jesus the example is Jesus the sacrifice for sin (cf. I Peter 2:18-25).

As Jesus is the model of righteousness, so the Devil is the model of sin. Whoever does sin belongs to the Devil, as he who does righteousness belongs to Christ. The Devil always has been a sinner. This does not mean the Devil always has been, as in Persian dualism, for the Devil himself was originally a creature of God. God did not create him as a Devil, so some form of a fall is necessary in monotheism. Of course the Devil can be dismissed in a process of demythologization, but he has a way of coming back as the depths of the demonic are faced. The Devil has power to deceive us into murdering and lying, but he has no power over Jesus (John 8:55; 14:30).

The couplet in the comment is perhaps a parenthesis to explain further why the Son of God is manifested in human flesh. He was manifested not only to bear away the sins of the world (3:5), but to destroy all the works of the Devil. Works in Johannine theology have reference to supernatural power. Jesus came to do the works of the Father (John 5:17; 9:4; 14:10), and he destroyed the works of the Devil. Conservative theology tends to think of the work of Christ in a Jesus versus God context, a view that makes Jesus a victim of God's punishment, and liberal theology has reacted in a Jesus versus man pattern that sees Jesus as human vicar who leads man to God. There is an element of truth in each, but early Christianity is vivid with a Jesus versus the Devil battle in which Jesus is victor over demonic powers.

This Jesus versus the Devil has been called the classic view of atonement in *Christus Victor,* an influential book by Gustaf Aulen. It is not difficult to support the Christus victor theme by appeal to the New Testament. The first half of the Gospel of Mark pictures Jesus as one in whom the Spirit invaded a demon infested world to cast out Satan. Satan as the strong one in his house is cast out by Jesus the stronger one who is the Son of God (3:20-27).[4] This view is by no means discarded in other New Testament writings (cf. Matthew 12:25-29; Luke 10:18; Acts 10:30; I Peter 3:22; Colossians 2:15; John 12:31). It is as hard to cast the Devil out of the New Testament as it was for ordinary men to cast him out of his house in human history!

The begetting of God's children explains their behavior (3:9). Those who have been begotten of God into a new life do not make a practice of sin. A false perfection has made havoc of the text by a failure to note the Greek tense. *Poiei* (does) is present indicative like *hamartanei* (sin) in 3:8, and the translation "does not make a practice of sin" attempts to bring this out. A. T. Robertson says: "The child of God does not have the habit of sin." C. H. Dodd

---

⁴ Moody, *Spirit of the Living God.* pp. 34-42.

thinks this may be too subtle, but the passage he appeals to assumes that the person who says "we have no sin" (1:8) is walking in darkness (1:6). To say we have no sin while walking in moral darkness is indeed self-deception. The tense in 2:1 is aorist, indicating single or occasional acts of sin, falling into sin, but the present indicative expresses continuous and habitual action. Anyone begotten of God may, under the stress of temptation, fall into sin, but he is unable to continue in sin while God's seed abides in him.

The meaning of God's seed abiding in him is a difficult question, but an answer must be sought. The various theories are expressed in the various translations. The seed (*sperma*) is interpreted as "offspring" in *A New Translation* (1913) by James Moffatt. Support for this is sought in the Old Testament usage of the story of the seed from Genesis 3:15 forward (cf. 17:9). Seed is often used in this sense in the New Testament (Luke 1:55; John 8:33,37; Galatians 3:16,29). Moffatt therefore said "the offspring of God remain in Him, and they cannot commit sin, because they are born of God." This is fascinating, but it is tautology, for remaining in God (Him) and not committing sin have the same meaning. Obviously, those who remain in fellowship with God do not commit sin, for sin would break this fellowship.

A second view interprets the seed as nature. This is vague and smacks of pagan mysticism, but it is adopted by both the *Revised Standard Version* and *Today's English Version*. In a Hermetic tractate, *On Regeneration*, the one to be initiated says: "I know not from what womb a man is born (again), and of what seed." Hermes replies: "My child, (the womb) is intellectual wisdom (conceiving) in silence, and the seed is the true Good" (*Corpus Hermeticum*, XIII. 1-2). The quotation is from C. H. Dodd, who tends to view Johannine theology against the pagan background, but he is not taken here as he is on the meaning of *chrisma* (anointment). His comment does throw light on those who think the seed is nature. He says: "The divine act of regeneration is thought (on analogy with the physical act) as implanting a divine principle from which the new nature of the children of God is produced." This sounds like much popular preaching, but this pagan concept is not satisfactory.

A third view is that the seed is the *logos* (word) of God. *The*

New English Bible (1962) translation of which C. H. Dodd was New Testament chairman, says "divine seed." This is the view of Dodd himself and apparently of most who reject the "offspring" and "nature" theories. The seed *(sperma)* is not mentioned again in I John, but there are several parallel statements that shed light on the statement that "his seed abides in him" in the sense that God's word abides in his begotten child and makes it impossible for one with the abiding word to continue in sin. Already the statements have been met: "the truth is not in us" (1:8), "his word *(logos)* is not in us" (1:10), "the word *(logos)* of God abides in you" (2:14), "the *chrisma* which you received from him abides in you" (2:27). Cf. 3:15,17,24; 4:13,15,16. *Alētheia* (truth), *logos* (word), *chrisma* (anointment), *sperma* (seed) sound very much the same, especially if the *chrisma* is imparted with the apostolic doctrine. The parallel between 2:14 and 3:9 is striking:

Ho logos tou theou en humin menei (the word of God abides in you)
Sperma autou en autōi menei (his seed abides in him).

The same idea is found at other stages of New Testament theology (Mark 4:14; Matthew 13:38-39; James 1:18; I Peter 1:23. Cf. I Corinthians 3:6; Acts 6:7; 9:17; 12:24; 16:5; 19:20; 28:30-31).

It is very difficult to determine whether 3:10 is a conclusion to what goes before or an introduction to what follows. In some sense it is both, for the first parallel points backward and the second points both backward and forward. It is a parenthetical bridge between the righteousness of God's children and the interpretation of righteousness in terms of brotherly love.

2. Keeping the commandments (3:10b-24).

(1) The commandment and the brother (3:10b-18).

10b Everyone who does not do righteousness is not of God,
    and any one who does not continue to love his brother;

11 because this is the message which you heard from the beginning,
    that we should continue to love one another;

12 and not be like Cain who was of the Evil One
and cut the throat of his brother.
>   (And for what reason did he cut his brother's throat?
>   Because his works were evil,
>>   but the works of his brother were righteous.

13   Do not marvel if the godless world hates you.

14   We know that we have passed from death into life
>   because we continue to love the brethren.
>>   Whoever does not continue to love abides
>>   in death).

15 Everyone who continues to hate his brother is a murderer;
>   and you know that no murderer has eternal life abiding
>   in him.

16   (By this we have come to know love,
>   because that One laid down his life,
>>   and we ought also to lay down our lives on
>>   behalf of the brethren.)

17 Whoever has the means of life in the godless world
and beholds his brother having need,
yet he shuts off compassion from him,
how does love for God abide in him?

18 Little children, let us not love in word nor with the tongue
but in work and with the truth.

This second part of keeping the commandments (3:10b-24) covers the same ground as the first (2:3-11), but from a different perspective. There are four couplets with a long parenthesis on the hate of Cain (3:10b-15) and a parenthesis followed by three couplets on the love of Christ (3:16-18). This analysis departs from that by J. C. O'Neill only at 3:18-19 where O'Neill overlooks a striking parallel and includes what better belongs to the next table (3:19-24). The Devil and God, darkness and light, death and life, hate and love, sin and righteousness, lie and truth, Cain and Christ illustrate the moral, not metaphysical, dualism of Johannine theology.

The first couplet (3:10b) indicates the close connection between the Johannine writings. He who does not love his brother does not do righteousness, for doing one is doing the other. This is very close to the Pauline teaching that love for the neighbor fulfills all the other commandments (Romans 13:9). John, therefore, speaks of the love commandment before he goes on to talk about commandments in the plural (3:22,24). The commandment and the commandments are used interchangeably (3:22-23).

The second couplet (3:11) makes clear that love for the brother is love for one another in the Christian fellowship. John does not speak about love for the neighbor and the enemy, although he would perhaps agree with Jesus and Paul, so the view of Rudolf Bultmann that John means the fellowman and the neighbor when he says brother is not acceptable. John means love for the Christian brother as a comparison of the first two couplets shows. The word *aggelia* (message) is found only twice in the New Testament (1:5; 3:11), but the statement that they had heard it "from the beginning" is a favorite Johannine phrase for that which is from the beginning of time or eternal (1:1; 2:7,13,14,24; 3:11). The same phrase was used in the other section on keeping the commandments (2:7).

Cain comes in to illustrate what lack of love for the brother can do and what it means in reference to one's relation to God. The deed of Cain was the work of the Evil One (cf. 2:13,14; 5:18), i.e., the Devil (3:8,10). A. T. Robertson points out that the old verb *sphazo* means "to slay, to butcher, to cut the throat (Latin *jugulare*) like an ox in the shambles" and that it is used only here and in Revelation (5:6,9,12,etc.). The above translation follows Robertson and *The Jerusalem Bible* (1966). This is a vivid detail about the fraticide of Genesis 4:1-16. It is often said this the only reference to the Old Testament in I John, but this is hardly true (cf. 2:1-2,5).

The parentheses have two triplets (3:12b,14) connected by a single line of exclamation (3:13). The first triplet is a further interpretation of Cain's hatred of his brother Abel. Wilder illuminates the motive of murder with a quotation from the *Testament of Gad* (4:6):

As love desires the quickening of the dead . . . ,
   so hate desires to put the living to death.

The living in I John are the righteous who rebuke the hateful by their example of brotherly love. A long passage in *The Wisdom of Solomon* portrays the resentment of the unrighteous for the righteous. Part of it says (2:12-16, *Revised Standard Version*):

> Let us lie in wait for the righteous man,
> because he is inconvenient to us and opposes our actions;
> he reproaches us for sin against the law,
> and accuses us of sins against our training.
> He professes to have knowledge of God,
> and calls himself a child of the Lord.
> He became to us a reproof of our thoughts;
> the very sight of him is a burden to us,
> because his manner of life is unlike that of others,
> and his ways are strange.
> We are considered by him as something base,
> and he avoids our ways as unclean;
> he calls the last end of the righteous happy,
> and boasts that God is his Father.

Unrighteousness is related to hate as righteousness is related to love. Abel is dead, but he is still a rebuke to the clan of Cain as well as an example of faith (cf. Hebrews 11:4).

The exclamation applies the murder of Abel by Cain to the conflict between those in the *koinōnia* with those still in the unredeemed *kosmos* (3:13). The brethren are again those who belong to the fellowship of light and love. The particular example from the Old Testament is seen as a general principle that explains the antipathy of the world for the righteous who translate righteousness into works of love. This is hardly evidence for persecution at the time of the writing, but it does explain the hatred of the world. Jesus said much the same in the High Priestly Prayer (John 17:14):

> I gave them thy word
> and the godless world hated them,
> because they are not of the godless world
> as I am not of the godless world.

The second triplet in the parentheses makes the positive approach to the example of Cain and draws from it assurance of eternal life

(3:14). A general heading for 3:12-16 in *The Centenary Transla-tion* (1924) speaks of "migrating from the Cain country to the Abel country," and, verse 14 is translated: "we know that we have migrated, out of death into life, because we love our brothers." A. T. Robertson sustains this translation with the observation that the same verb is used when the brothers of Jesus said to him: "Leave here and go to Judea" (John 7:3). The same tense is used when Jesus says one who believes in him "has passed from death to life" (John 5:24). The life is here the eternal life of God imparted to man through Christ. As long as one has Christ, he has this eternal life (5:12), but he may turn from Christ and commit the sin of idolatry that leads to death (5:16,21). If one does not love his brother, he has not passed over into the realm of eternal life.

One may abide in death as well as life (3:14). Abiding in death is abiding in darkness, hate, unrighteousness, and in the clutches of the Evil One (cf. 5:18). This is spiritual death here and now as eternal life is spiritual life possessed already through the mediation of Christ.

The fourth couplet (3:15) resumes the argument that hate is the basic motive of murder. Jesus taught that hatred was murder al-ready (Matthew 5:21-22). The word for murderer is *anthrōpok-tonos*, a word found in the New Testament only here and in John 8:44 where the Devil is said to be "a murderer from the beginning and has nothing to do with the truth, because there is no truth in him." The desire to kill Jesus by those who claimed to be heirs of Abraham only revealed that their father was the Devil (John 8:44). As the Evil One, the Devil, inspired Cain, so he moved in the hearts who hated Jesus. Cain is for John what Adam is for Paul.

No murderer has eternal life, for he who would take the life of a brother does not have the attitude of heart to receive God's life. The taking of life and the receiving of life are mutually exclusive. A murderer prefers a murderer to Christ (cf. Acts 3:14-15). He abides in death, and it is axiomatic that he who abides in death does not have eternal life abiding in him. Hate and death belong together as do love and life.

The love of Christ contrasts with the hate of Cain (3:16-18). A parenthesis in triplet form expounds Christ's sacrifice of his own life as an example of supreme love for the brethren (3:16), and this is followed by three couplets of exhortation for the secondary sacrifice of this world's goods to meet human need and thus expressing human love for God (3:17). Cain's hate is an example of the taking of life, while the sacrifice of Christ and Christians is the giving of eternal life and the sustaining of earthly life. Reverence for life, both eternal and earthly, could hardly be stated more simply and sublimely.

The knowledge of *agapē* is introduced with the same *en toutōi* (by this) noticed at the beginning of the first section on keeping the commandments (2:3-11). This is a favorite transitional phrase in I John (cf. 2:5; 3:10,19,24; 4:9,13,17). Love is literally "the love" as life is "the life." The One is again *ekeinos* (cf. 2:6; 3:3,5), and it seems always to mean Christ. This is certainly the case when it is said "that One laid down his life on behalf of the brethren."

The Greek preposition *hyper* has been translated literally "on behalf of" rather than with the weaker "for," because both *anti,* literally in the place of, and *hyper* are translated by the one preposition "for" in many translations. This fails to make the distinction between the vicarious sacrifice, which may also be exemplary, and the less frequent *anti* which is substitutionary (Mark 10:45; I Timothy 2:6). Even *anti* may be used in the context of the exemplary (cf. Mark 10:41-45).

If this seems unnecessary emphasis on prepositions, let it be remembered that advocates of penal substitution have often looked upon any emphasis on the death of Christ as an example of some unworthy taint of "liberalism." The death of Christ as the supreme example of sacrificial love belongs to every level of New Testament teaching (I Peter 2:21; 3:18; I Corinthians 11:1; II Corinthians 8:9; 10:1; Galatians 2:20; Hebrews 12:3-4; I Thessalonians 1:6; 2:20; 6:2; Philippians 2:2-8; I Timothy 6:13), but this is the special language of Johannine theology.

The following passages on vicarious love have had enormous influence on all Christian groups: the parable of the good shepherd, the unconscious prophecy of Caiaphas, the denial of Peter, and the sayings on love for friends (10:11,15; 11:50; 13:37-38; 15:13). Very few in these times are called upon to make this supreme sacrifice, but that may not be a credit to contemporary Christianity. It must have been exalting to be Christians when Paul could say of two Jewish Christians: "Greet Prisca and Aquila, my fellow workers in Christ Jesus, who risked their necks for my life, to whom all the churches of the Gentiles give thanks; greet also the church in their house" (Romans 16:4).

The practical application of love in meeting human need turns from eternal life in the last couplet (3:15) to earthly life in the next three (3:17-18). The means of life in this godless *kosmos* is *bios*. The vain-glory of *bios* has already been rejected (2:16), but the needs of this *bios* are not to be ignored. Human life on earth needs to be sustained before the heavenly life is fully inherited. Indifference to these human needs has often brought the church into disrepute and led to opposition, and the present time is ripe for revolution in most so-called Christian lands.

Compassion for all men is a New Testament teaching, but I John is concerned primarily for the brother in need. This also belongs to the earliest days of the church. Clothing and food for a poor brother was an essential for saving faith (James 2:14-17). Compassion is concern tempered by love. The word for compassion (*splagchna*) is found only here in the Johannine writings, but it is found also in Paul (Philippians 2:1; Colossians 3:12).

Compassion for a brother in need is evidence that one has love for God. He who shuts the door of his heart in the presence of need shuts out God as well as his brother. Love for God does not abide where love for the brother is absent. Love for God is one of those abiding things in the heart of a true Christian (cf. 1:8,10; 2:27; 3:15, 17,24; 4:13,15,16). Lack of compassion was one of the changes brought against the Docetics by Ignatius of Antioch. He says: "Pay close attention to those who have wrong notions about the grace of Jesus Christ, which has come to us, and note how at variance they are with God's mind. They care nothing about love: they have no concern for widows and orphans, for the oppressed, for those in prison or released, for the hungry or the thirsty" (*Smyrneans* 6:2).

The parallel of the last couplet is a conclusion to the section on the commandment and the brother and a transition to the commandments and God (3:17). The empty sham of a religion that involves nothing more than word and the tongue is rebuked against the background of the way of the deed and truth as expressions of Christian love. "Here is a case where actions do speak louder than mere words" (A. T. Robertson). Truth becomes the link word for the next section where "of the truth" means we have our source of life in truth.

(2) The commandments and God (3:19-24).

19 By this we shall know that we are of the truth
   and shall persuade our heart before him,
20   (even if our heart blames us)

   because God is greater than our heart
   and knows all things.

21 Beloved, if the heart does not blame us,
   we have confidence with God;

22 and whatever we ask
   we receive from him,

   because we are keeping his commandments
   and we are doing what is pleasing before him.

23 (And this is his commandment,
   in order that we should believe in the name of his Son
        Jesus Christ
             and love one another just as he gave a
                commandment to us).

24 Whoever goes on keeping his commandments abides in him
   and he in him;

   and by this we know that he abides in us,
   by the Spirit whom he gave to us.

As the section on keeping the commandments turns from the singular only (commandment) to include the plural (commandments), a nest of problems in translation and interpretation is confronted. C. H. Dodd has well called the first four lines (3:19-20) "a notorious *crux interpretum*," and many solutions have been proposed. J. C. O'Neill puts 3:19a in one table and 3:19b in another, but the parallel of future tenses ("we shall know . . . we shall persuade") seems too close for that arrangement. The larger parallel of knowing we are of the truth and persuading our heart in the presence of God increases the probability of the above arrangement. The biggest problem is what to do with the awkward statement, "even if our heart blames us," translated as literally as possible and put in parentheses. J. C. O'Neill seems correct to the extent that this is a comment, but his theory that the rest is a pre-Christian hymn is not accepted. The conditional comment in the positive seems to anticipate the negative in the next verse. If this is not correct, then the double use of *hoti* (that or because) is redundant. Moffatt tried to solve the problem with "whenever" (cf. *The Centenary Translation* and *Revised Standard Version),* and A. T. Robertson came forth with "whereinsoever," but appeal to John 2:5 and 14:13 by the latter does not convince. *The Jerusalem Bible* says "whatever" and Barclay "when." The simple "for if" in *Today's English Version* is also good in smooth English, but "even if" seems best *(New English Bible).*

The meaning of 3:19 may point back to loving in deed and in truth as the ground of reassurance for the troubled heart, but it more likely points to the great love of God's knowing concern that follows. This is the usual use of "by this" *(en toutōi,* 2:3,5; 3:10; 4:2,9,10, 17). The all-knowing love of God is the ground on which the troubled heart will come to know and come to be persuaded before God at the final judgment. The future tenses may also have reference to future times of troubled thoughts before the final judgment, but confidence *(parrēsia)* has elsewhere been related to the coming *(parousia)* of God in judgment (2:28; 3:21). Peter saw this all-knowing love in the risen Jesus (John 21:17). Paul was willing to rest all on the belief that the critical judgment of others and even his own self-judgment must await God's final judgment (I Corinthians 4:1-5). Those who know little love little. God is greater in knowledge because he is greater in love, and he who knows all loves all.

There is much background to this concept of God's all-knowing love. The Psalmist said (103:13-14):

> As a father pities his children,
>> so the LORD pities those who fear him.

> For he knows our frame;
>> he remembers that we are dust.

A hymn from Qumran looks upon God as the source of truth and

takes comfort in God's knowledge in a cluster of other concepts
(*The Book of Hymns*, 11:3-14, tr. Theodor H. Gaster):

> For I know that Thy mouth is truth,
> and in Thy hand is bounty,
> and in Thy thought all knowledge,
> and in Thy power all might,
> and that all glory is with Thee.

In the Pauline writings God's knowledge and God's love are closely
associated, and this helps to understand the parallels in I John 3:19-
20 (cf. I Corinthians 8:2-3; 13:12; Galatians 4:9).

A very old view goes back to the Greek fathers, and it is still
heard in the pulpits of traditional churches. The argument is advanced that if the heart knows things against the believer, then the
great God knows even more, and if the heart condemns one, then
God condemns even more. This preaching is intended to dispel
complacency and to "produce conviction of sin," and it has often
led to extreme forms of penance in Catholicism and penitence in
Protestantism. This is a possible interpretation in the light of the
difficult textual problems, but it perhaps misses the comfort of God's
all-knowing love. Guilt hardly needs to be "produced." The great
need of guilty hearts is reassurance that God in his love will forgive
(cf. 2:1-2,12).

The next four verses, as the text now stands, follow a trinitarian
pattern, but it may be that an earlier edition had a monotheism of
God and his Spirit. This would not be unusual, for the New Testament faith moved from monothesim (the belief in one God) through
binitarianism (the belief in a unique relation between the Father
and the Son) to trinitarianism (the unity of Father, Son and Holy
Spirit in one being).

GOD (3:21-22).

The more frequent form of address has thus far been little children (*teknia*, 2:1,12,28; 3:7,18. Cf. 4:4; 5:21), but young children
(*paidia*, 2:14,18) and beloved (*agapētoi*, 2:7, 3:2) have appeared.
It seems that the approaching theme of love leads to a frequency of
the term beloved (3:21; 4:1,7,11. Cf. III John 1,2,5,11).

God's love gives the persuaded heart *parrēsia* (confidence, freedom to speak). Both *The New English Bible* and *The Jerusalem Bible* translate *kardia* as conscience, but this is confusing. Conscience is a very important concept in the New Testament, but it translates the Stoic word *syneidēsis* and has a more limited meaning than *kardia* (cf. I Peter 3:16,19,21; Hebrews 9:9,14; 10:2,22; I Corinthians 8:7,10; 10:25,27,28,29; II Corinthians 1:12; 4:2; 5:11; Romans 2:15; 9:1; 13:5; I Timothy 3:9; II Timothy 1:3; Titus 1:15; Acts 23:1). *Kardia* is a Hebrew concept for the inner life of man (emotional, volitional, mental). It translates the Hebrew *leb* in the Septuagint. The moral function of conscience is included in the functions of the heart, but the meaning is narrowed when conscience and heart are made synonyms.

The accusation of the heart is expressed with a word found elsewhere in the New Testament only in Galatians 2:11 where Paul says Peter "stood condemned" *(kategnōsmenos ēn)*. As Paul blamed Peter for his inconsistency, so the human heart knows things against the troubled believer (3:19), but the believer is beloved by an all-knowing God and an all-forgiving fellowship, so there is freedom to speak one's mind before God and man. This freedom to speak *(parrēsia,* confidence) at the coming *(parousia)* of God in final judgment (2:28) may also be applied to prayer in the present. This is powerfully stated in an exhortation in Hebrews: "Let us then with confidence *(parrēsia)* draw near to the throne of grace, that we may have mercy and find grace to help in time of need" (4:16). The next verse (3:22) makes plain that this form of "realized eschatology" is present now.

This confidence in prayer was a cardinal teaching of Jesus. "Therefore, I tell you, whatever you ask in prayer, believe you will receive, and you will" (Mark 11:24. Cf. Luke 11:9). This may sound very easy out of context, but it leads to Gethsemane when put into practice (Mark 14:32-42). Prayer belonged to the most crucial moments in the life of Jesus and Luke paints seven moving portraits of Jesus as the paragon of prayer (3:21 5:6; 6:12; 9:18,28f; 11:1; 22:44).

The two parallelisms on prayer have first "we ask—we receive," but there is a rhyming in the Greek between "we are keeping" and "we are doing." The "him" each time is God (cf. 1:5; 2:3,27,28,29; 3:6). From "him" we receive and before "him" our deeds are pleasing. Pleasing God, as Jesus pleased God, is part of Paul's teaching (Romans 12:2; 15:3,16), and the beautiful benediction in Hebrews has enshrined it in worship (13:20-21). Keeping his commandments pleases God, and the summary of the commandments is love.

HIS SON (3:23).

A triplet suddenly appears among couplets, and J. C. O'Neill may be right in seeing this as a later edition to give Christian clarity to the meaning of keeping the commandments. The plural (commandments) is suddenly interpreted with the singular (commandment), then there is a return to the plural again (3:24). This must not be pushed too far, since O'Neill's analysis has both the plural and the singular in the same source in the first section on keeping the commandments (2:3-11).

The content makes the triplet distinctly Christian. There is one commandment containing a unity of believing and behaving. Believing on the name of his son Jesus Christ and loving one another are one commandment. A dozen more declarations are found in I John (1:5; 2:25; 3:11; 4:3,21; 5:3,4,6,9,11,14,20). Believing is met here for the first time in I John. Believing is a noun only once in I John (5:4). The rest of the time it is verbal action (3:23; 4:1,16; 5:1,5,10,13). The content of faith is expressed as that which is confessed (2:23; 4:2-3,15), so it is false to make a radical distinction between the act and the content of faith.

Believing always has an object. Belief in believing is not Johannine! Here the object of believing is "the name of his Son Jesus Christ." The name means the person, a concept found hundreds of times in the Old Testament. Believing in a proposition is not the same as believing in a person. Believing in a person is trust, and trust is always an I-Thou relation. Propositional statements may indeed be made about this relationship. We may "believe the love God has for us" (4:16), "that Jesus is the Son of God" (5:5), "the testimony that God has borne to his Son" (5:10) as well as "in the Son of God" (5:10) or "in the name of the Son of God" (5:13). Believing "in his name" is believing "in him" (John 1:12; 2:23; 3:18).

Son expresses a unique relationship between God and Jesus Christ. This Father-Son relationship is the basis of both fellowship and

faith. He who has Christian fellowship has "fellowship with the
Father and with his Son Jesus Christ" (1:3), and the liar is one who
denies this relationship (2:22-24). He who abides in this doctrine
"has both the Father and the Son" (II John 9). The unity of Christians is based upon and like unto the unity between the Father and
the Son (John 17:3,10-11), but the relationship of Christians with
God is always, in Johannine theology, a Father-children relationship. The Father-Son relationship exists between God and Jesus
Christ alone. He is "the only Son of God" (John 3:16).[5]

Believing in his Son and brotherly love are one commandment
in this parenthetical comment, but the new commandment is usually
confined to love for one another (John 13:34; 15:12-17). The
Gnostics neither believed in his Son Jesus Christ nor loved one another. Their withdrawal from the fellowship was logical (2:19).
The High Priestly Prayer has these words on the lips of Jesus: "I
made known thy name, and I will make it known, that the love with
which thou hast loved me may be in them, and I in them" (John
17:26). Johannine Christology and ecclesiology are inseparable.
This is not the first nor the last time that this mutual love is the
flower of Christian faith (3:11; 4:7).

HIS SPIRIT (3:24).

Keeping the commandments is a sign that one abides in God, but
this relationship is two-sided. God abides in those who abide in
God (cf. 4:13,15). He (autos) can only mean God, for it refers to
"his commandments" and "him." If it had reference to Jesus Christ,
John would perhaps say "that One" (ekeinos, 3:3,5,7,16; 4:17). This
is again God-mysticism. As God perfectly indwelt Jesus in the
incarnation, he progressively indwells those who keep God's commandments (John 14:10,17), but the indwelling of the Father is the
indwelling of the Son (John 14:23). The Father and the Son in
inseparable union make their abode (14:23, monē, home) in the
same heart. As Jesus prayed, these relations were all brought into
focus: "I in them and thou in me, that they may be perfectly one,
so that the world may know that thou hast sent me and hast loved
them as thou has loved me" (John 17:23).

---

[5] Dale Moody, "God's Only Son," *Journal of Biblical Literature*, LXXII, pt. IV (Dec.,
1953), pp. 213-19.

God's abiding in us may be known. Up to the phrase "by the Spirit whom he gave us," it would seem keeping God's commandments is the basis of this knowledge that one abides in God and God abides in him, but the final phrase introduces a new element into the passage. J. C. O'Neill says this final phrase is an editorial comment, but this destroys the parallelism of God's abiding in us and God's gift of the Spirit. The *chrisma* has already been discussed in terms of God's Spirit (2:20,27), but the word first appears in I John here (3:24). The word *pneuma* appears later in three very significant settings (4:1-6,13; 5:6-12), and the second is almost an exact parallel to the phrase in 3:24. The adjective Holy does not appear with Spirit in I John and Revelation.

The view of the Spirit in this final phrase, however, is the same as that in the Gospel of John. John's Gospel has six passages on the Spirit before Jesus is glorified by death and resurrection (1:32-33; 3:3-8,34; 4:23-24; 6:63; 7:29) and six that speak of the ministry of the Spirit after his glorification (14:15-17,25-26; 15:26-27; 16:4b-11, 12-15; 20:22). This marks the beginning of the eschatological community in which the present possession of the Spirit is the promise of God for the all future fulfillment. It is the mutual indwelling of the Father and the Son among those who keep the commandment of mutual love.

3. Guarding against the enemy in the godless *kosmos* (4:1-6): false prophets.

> 1 Beloved, do not believe every spirit,
> > but test the spirits to see whether they are of God;
> > > for many false prophets have gone out into the godless world.

> 2 (By this you know the Spirit of God:
> > every Spirit which confesses that Jesus Christ has come in the flesh is of God,
> 3 and every spirit which does not confess Jesus is not of God.

> And this is the spirit of Antichrist,
> > which you have heard that it is coming,
> > > and now it is in the godless world already.)

4 You are of God, little children,
　　and you have overcome them,
　　　　for greater is the One who is in you than the One who
　　　　　　is in the godless world.

5 They are of the godless world,
　　therefore what they say is of the godless world,
　　　　and the godless world listens to them.

6　　　　　We are of God:
　　whoever knows God listens to us;
　　　　whoever is not of God does not listen to us.
　　(From this we know the spirit of truth and the spirit of error.)

The address of beloved is used for a third time (2:7; 3:21; 4:1),
and belief is used again in the sense of trust (3:23; 4:1). There is
also the idea of acknowledgement and recognition. Spirit *(pneuma)*
is the link word between the second section on keeping the commandments (3:10b-24) and this second section on guarding against
the Antichrist (4:1-6). The connection is so close that William
Barclay makes 3:24b-4:1 a unit on "The Perils of the Surging Life
of the Spirit," but 4:1-6 has long been recognized as "a self-contained
section" (J. C. O'Neill). In the first part, overcoming the godless
world (2:12-17) and guarding against the antichrists (2:18-24) are
separate sections, but the two topics are now merged in one section
on guarding against the antichrists in the godless *kosmos.* As the
text now stands, there is a balance between testing the false
prophets (4:1-3) and triumphing over them (4:4-6). There are
three triplets in each, but J. C. O'Neill may be right in his argument
for an earlier edition of twelve lines. Later additions are in parentheses.

A triplet swarming with spirits may seem strange in a day when
many would demythologize even the teaching on the transcendent
Spirit of God, but the ideas of antichrists and the Antichrist make
sense only when this *plērōma* of supernatural spirits is presupposed.
A *plērōma* is the totality of supernatural powers (cf. Colossians
2:9) as a pantheon includes all the gods. The term, used several
times in Pauline writings, is found only once in the Johannine writings (John 1:16), but the idea is behind the concept of spirits.

Testing the spirits (4:1) comes at false prophets like a metallurgist testing coins. A true prophet stands the test (*dokimos*, cf. II Corinthians 10:18), but the false prophet is rejected (*adokimos*, I Corinthians 9:27; II Corinthians 13:5-7). The true prophet dominates the second section of the Old Testament canon, but there is ever the recognition of false prophets. They are exposed in a dramatic way by Micaiah in the former prophets (I Kings 22), and the caustic criticism of Jeremiah is a climax of the protests of the latter prophets (Jeremiah 14:14). Jeremiah reflects the Deuteronomic test (Deuteronomy 13:1-5). *The Dead Sea Scriptures* warn against "prophets of deceit" and "lying prophets" (*Hymns* 4:5-40).

John the Baptist was a prophet and more than a prophet (Matthew 12:9; Luke 7:28), but Jesus had some severe warnings against false prophets and even false Christs (Matthew 7:15; 24:11,24). True prophets flourished in the New Testament churches (Acts 11:27-28; 13:1-3; 21:9-12; Revelation 16:13; 19:20; 20:10; II Peter 2:1). False prophets appear in the Pauline letters and they are recognized by their rejection of Jesus (I Corinthians 12:3), but there is a liberty of prophecy and tongues, under certain regulations, in Paul's teachings that would arouse complacent churches of the present (I Corinthians 14). A little hymn in Paul's first letter represents the balance between freedom and order in the New Testament times (I Thessalonians 5:16-22).[6]

Tongues do not appear in the Johannine writings, but they are in agreement with Paul on prophecy. Prophets are free to prophesy, but they must be tested. Prophecy in itself is no proof that they belong to God. It may be that an evil spirit is speaking through a false prophet, as Satan may later appear in the Antichrist. The phrase "of God" (*ek theou*), used seven times in seven verses (4:1-7), means "that the person, spirit, or the quality *has its source and origin in God*" (William Barclay). It has been translated literally the same each of the six times in the above section.

The false prophets have gone out of the *koinōnia* of light and love into the *kosmos* of darkness and hate. A. T. Robertson says the perfect active indicative (*exelēluthasin*) means "they are abroad always," and he rightly relates this to the aorist (*exēlthan*, they went out) in the first section on the antichrists (2:19). They went out from the fellowship because they gave up the faith. Those who are

---

[6] Dale Moody, *Spirit of the Living God*, pp. 86f.

no longer "with us" soon go out "from us" (note the further comments on 2:19). Both conduct and doctrine are tests in II John.

This problem of false prophets continued to trouble the church after New Testament times. A second century church manual called the *Didache,* a writing that verged on making the canon in Alexandria, has also some very specific rules other than doctrine by which false prophets can be detected (chs. 11-12). A crisis was reached when Montanus (in the last half of the second century) apparently confused himself with the Paraclete (the Holy Spirit) and stampeded the institutional church into a rigidity against prophetic preaching from which recovery has not yet been reached. Biblical balance is hard to retain under the restraints of ecclesiastical tradition.

A comment turns from the crisis caused by the false prophets to the criterion by which they may be recognized (4:2-3). This is another of the statements of recognition that begin with "by this" (*en toutōi*), (2:3,5; 3:10,16,19; 4:2,9,13,17). How is one to distinguish inspiration that has its source in the Spirit of God from that which belongs to the Antichrist? The Spirit of God is "the Spirit which God gave to us" (3:24), "his own Spirit" (4:13), and the Spirit which is "the witness" and "the truth" (5:7-8).

That to which the Spirit bears witness is twofold. God's Spirit first of all is the witness that Jesus is the Christ. This was the special emphasis of the first section on guarding against antichrists (2:22-23). The joining of the word Jesus, the human name, with the Christ, the representative of God, refutes the Jewish element in this heresy of Hellenistic Jewish Christianity. Jesus is the Anointed, the Messiah, in whom all the promises of God find their yes, as Paul would express it (II Corinthians 1:20). All three of the Synoptic Gospels speak of Jesus' anointment with the Spirit after his baptism, and the Gospel of John leaves out direct reference to water baptism altogether as he speaks of the descent of the Spirit as a dove from heaven upon the historical Jesus (1:29-34).

The second fact to which the Spirit of God bears witness is incarnation, i.e., "that Jesus Christ has come in the flesh." This refutes the Hellenistic element in the Gnostic heresy. Plato's hair would probably have stood on end had he heard John say "the word became flesh" (John I:14). The flesh to a Greek dualist like Plato and the later Gnostics was evil, a thing from which man was to be redeemed rather than a means of redemption. The Gnostics no doubt exploded on reading such passages as: "Truly, truly, I say to you, unless you eat the flesh of the Son of man and drink his blood, you have no life in you; he who eats my flesh and drinks my blood has eternal life, and I will raise him up at the last day. For my flesh is food indeed, and my blood is drink indeed. He who eats of my flesh and drinks of my blood abides in me, and I in him" (John 6:53-56).

As Gnosticism reached its blooming time toward the end of the second century, three great anti-Gnostic theologians built a wall against the heresy by developing in detail the three fundamentals of creation, incarnation, and the resurrection of the body. The practical application of these fundamentals was appeal to an apostolic creed, clergy, and canon, and this took the form of the Apostles' Creed, Apostolic Succession, and the New Testament Canon of apostolic writings. The Apostles' Creed follows the pattern of the three fundamentals.[7]

Confession of belief in the incarnation is the connecting word between the members of the parallel (4:2-3). This is obscured by a textual variation which has usually been translated "every spirit which divides Jesus." The Latin Vulgate reflects this reading with the translation *solvit,* but modern scholars do not accept this reading. It is true that the Gnostics sought to divide Jesus from the Christ, but this is not what the best manuscripts say. Otto Piper has shown, in any case, that the Greek reading *luei* had the meaning to exorcise or anathematize.[8] This would agree with Paul's confession (I Corinthians 12:3).

The content of the confession distinguishes the working of God's Spirit from the Antichrist. The word spirit does not appear in the Greek phrase translated "the spirit of Antichrist," but it is implied by the presence of the neuter article *to.* This radical distinction between those who confess belief in the incarnation and those who do not may sound harsh to the modern reader, but it should be remembered that the life of Christianity was threatened by this growing Gnosticism.

The Antichrist is the same as that noted in the first polemical

---

[7] This is set forth with great clarity in Anders Nygren, *Agape and Eros* (Philadelphia: Westminster Press, 1953), pp. 235-446.

[8] *Journal of Biblical Literature,* LXVI (1947), pp. 443-444.

section (2:18). This is another of the great declarations (1:5; 2:25; 3:11,23; 4:3,21; 5:3,4,6,9,11,14,20). Rudolf Bultmann says the apocalyptic idea of a coming Antichrist has been demythologized and historicized by identification with the Gnostic heresy, but this is hardly correct. The spirit of Antichrist is already at work in the godless *kosmos* as the Spirit of God is already at work in the *koinōnia*, but there is still a *parousia* of the Evil One, the Devil, as there is a *parousia* of God (2:28. Cf. II Thessalonians 2:8-10). The two ideas are radically related to the present crisis, but they are not demythologized.

The triumph over the false prophets is a victory over the spirit of Antichrist (4:4-6). This is set forth with three triplets and a summary comment. The first triplet (4:4) speaks of the readers as having their "source and origin in God" (*ek tou theou* now for the fourth time in this section). This relationship to God is further reinforced by the address of little children (*teknia* for the sixth of the seven times it is used in the letter, cf. 2:1 for references).

Those overcome by the little children are the false prophets who have gone forth from the *koinōnia* into the godless *kosmos* (4:1). The false prophets are in the godless *kosmos*, so they are overcome when the *kosmos* of unredeemed humanity is overcome. The verb *nenikēkate* has already been used in the first section on overcoming the godless *kosmos* to describe the victory of the believers called young men (2:14). The victory of the young men was over the Evil One, the Devil, but "the whole godless world lies in the Evil One" (5:19). This is a victory of faith. The little children are later described as those who have "been begotten of God" and who overcome the godless *kosmos* because they believe "that Jesus is the Son of God" (5:4-5). As Jesus overcame the godless *kosmos* in conflict and by way of the cross, so now his disciples are assured of a like victory (cf. John 16:33).

The victory of the little children over the godless *kosmos* is due to the presence of God. It was the *logos* (word) of God that was said to give strength to the young men of the first section (2:14), but now the strength of the little children is attributed to God himself ("the One who is in you"). See the comments on 3:9 for those things which are said to be or to abide in God's children. Later statements in this chapter clarify the implication that it is God's presence in his children that gives them victory (4:13,15,16). The

One in the godless *kosmos* is the Evil One (2:13,14; 3:12; 5:18,19). This is the solid food of moral dualism that is hard for modern moralists to digest, but that was John's Ephesian menu. The context would allow for the translation in *Today's English Version* in which the first One is the Spirit of truth and the second is the spirit of error.

The next two triplets were recognized as powerful poetic parallelism in *A New Translation* (1913) by James Moffatt. The first describes the false prophets (4:5). They have their source and origin in the *kosmos (ek tou kosmou)*. This is the godless *kosmos* characterized as "the lust of the flesh and the lust of the eyes and the vainglory of life" (2:16). It is also the world of hate that is hostile toward those who live in the *koinōnia* of brotherly love (3:13). This does not mean that the godless *kosmos* is beyond redemption, for Jesus Christ is the sacrifice for the sins of "the whole *kosmos*" (2:2) and "the Savior of the *kosmos*" (4:14), but the false prophets are hostile antichrists who have gone out from the *koinōnia* and set themselves against those who believe in the incarnation.

Their teaching also has its source and origin in the *kosmos (ek tou kosmou)*. They do not teach the apostolic belief of Jesus as the Christ who was flesh of our flesh. Their Christ was only idea that could not be touched (cf. 1:1). He, the Gnostic idea of Christ, could not redeem men because he never became a man among men. The incarnation of the eternal *Logos* is distinctly Christian (John 1:14), although it is based on belief in God's good creation in the Old Testament (Genesis 1:1-2:4a). The eternal has appeared in the concrete reality of human flesh. That the Gnostics could not accept. God had revealed to mere babes what "the wise and understanding" were unable to grasp (cf. Matthew 11:25).

The godless *kosmos* heard the Gnostics gladly, for the Gnostics preached it as the godless *kosmos* "had always heard it." Hundreds of years before, Heraclitus of Ephesus had spoken of a *Logos* that abides through all the flux of nature, but he did not say that it would one day become flesh. A long tradition was on the side of the Gnostics, and tradition is hard for even truth to uproot. No doubt many a disciple was tempted to give his ear to "good Greek philosophy" and "get relevant" with "modern man," but Presbyter John would call them back to the belief that "the *Logos* became flesh and dwelt among us" (John 1:14). He was interested in something more vital than "getting a hearing" from those with an appetite for Gnostic hash.

The parallel triplet puts Presbyter John himself among the little children who have their source and origin in God (*ek tou theou* again!). This is echoed in the High Priestly Prayer of John's Gospel. "I have given them your word (*logos*); and the *kosmos* had hated them because they are not of the *kosmos* (*ek tou kosmou*), even as I am not of the *kosmos* (*ek tou kosmou*). I do not pray that you should take them out of the *kosmos* (*ek tou kosmou*), but that you should keep them from the Evil One. They are not of the *kosmos* (*ek tou kosmou*) as I am not of the *kosmos* (*ek tou kosmou*) (John 17:14-16).

The sharp distinction between those who are *ek tou kosmou* and those who are *ek tou theou* is not some theory of predestination based on irresistible grace, as C. H. Dodd seems to fear. It is a very practical observation and explanation as to why some leave the *koinōnia* with the false prophets or antichrists. Those who keep renewing their acquaintance with God turn away from Gnosticism and cleave to the apostolic faith. The meaning of the phrase "whoever knows God" is well summarized by A. T. Robertson who says it means keeping "in tune with the Infinite God." Whoever knows God "is the one who keeps on getting acquainted with God, growing in the knowledge of God." This interpretation is based upon the careful attention Robertson gave to the present active participle. It makes all "the difference in the world" in I John when the Greek tenses are kept in mind.

Those who have their source and origin in God and keep on drinking from the source keep coming back for more of the apostolic preaching of Presbyter John. Those cut off from the source by foolish following of the false prophets go away to hear something more "spiritual" than a gospel that says "Jesus Christ has come to the flesh." It is amazing how contemporary this conflict of faiths sounds. There are so many today who think palaver about a "Christ idea" or a "Christ event" has a "depth" that "the man Christ Jesus" does not have. It may have a "depth" not found in the theology of incarnation, but it is a demonic depth.

The final comment in this section is a summary that is often compared to the teachings about the two spirits in *The Dead Sea Scriptures* of Qumran (*The Manual of Discipline*, 3:13-4:26), but there is a great difference as well as a similarity. A deterministic dualism dominates the teachings in Qumran. Both spirits are in the heart of each man in Qumran, while one is in the *koinōnia* and the other is in the *kosmos* in I John. Qumran is nearer to Paul's teachings on the two desires in man (cf. Galatians 5:16-17), but not even Paul's doctrine of predestination has the dualism of Qumran. *The Testament of Judah* has almost an exact parallel to the parenthetical comment in I John 4:6. In ccntext, it says (20:1-2):

> Know, therefore, my children, that two spirits wait upon man,
>   the spirit of truth and the spirit of error.
> And in the midst is the spirit of understanding of the mind,
>   to which it belongs to turn whithersoever it will.

The "from this," not the usual "by this" would not have been addressed to God's little children as a warning if a deterministic doctrine of predestination were in John's mind. Dualistic determinism infected Christianity through the Manicheanism behind Augustine's interpretation of predestination, but is it not in the New Testament.[9]

---

[9] My commentary on Romans, chs. 7-11, in the *Broadman Bible Commentary*, attempts to justify this statement.

Chapter 5

COMMENTARY ON THE FIRST LETTER OF JOHN

LOVE (4:7-5:21).

1. Keeping the commandment (4:7-21).

  (1) Manifested love (4:7-11).

7 Beloved, let us love one another;
    (for love is of God),
        and everyone who loves has been begotten of God
         (and knows God);

8   whoever does not love does not know God,
           (for God is love.)

9 (By this was the love of God manifested in us,
    because God has sent his only Son into the godless world
      in order that we might live through him.

10 By this is love,
    not that we have loved God, but that he loved us
      and sent his Son to be an expiation concerning
        our sins.

11 Beloved, since God so loved us,
    we also ought to love one another.)

Keeping the commandments followed the sections on avoiding sin in parts one and two (2:3-11; 3:10b-24), but it has moved now into first place in the third part. Love has come to dominate this part as light and life did the first two, and this explains why keeping the commandment of love has been made so prominent. Many would extend the section on love as far as 5:5. This is possible, and it would add a fifth section which could be called victorious love (5:1-5), but it seems more like a transition from love to faith as the third section on overcoming the godless *kosmos* is introduced. In broad outline this section on keeping the commandment of love may be divided into four subsections: manifested love (4:7-11), abiding love (4:12-16), perfect love (4:17-18), and brotherly love (4:19-21).

The subsection on manifested love has been divided into an older source and a distinctively Christian comment by J. C. O'Neill. This has been indicated by the parentheses (4:9-11), but it is doubtful that sectarian Judaism composed the lofty lines on loving one another (4:7-8). It may be that the three clauses in parentheses at 4:7-9 are comments (cf. R. Bultmann). It is possible that it influenced the original Christian composition to which a combative comment has been added in order to refute the rising heresy of Gnosticism out of the background of Gnostic Judaism. The reference to twelve disciples of John the Baptist (Acts 19:1-7) and later to "fierce wolves" among the flock at Ephesus (Acts 20:29) may be of more significance than is commonly recognized. C. H. Dodd has quoted passages from the *Corpus Hermeticum* to show how Hellenism could speak of a God "whose nature is to create, rule, and judge, but not to love."

The first six lines do appeal to God's eternal being as the basis for obedience to the love commandment. A Gnostic could go that far in his religious confession and stop short of God's historical action in Jesus Christ so powerfully stated in the next six lines that O'Neill has designated as Christian polemic against sectarian Judaism. As the text now stands, God's eternal being and God's historical action give two reasons for keeping the great commandment of love.

God's eternal being is the source of love (4:7). The great phrase "of God" (*ek tou theou*) was prominent in the previous section on guarding against the enemy as manifested in many antichrists

or false prophets. It is used for the seventh time in seven verses,
but now it designates God as eternal being and the fountain from
which all love flows. Gnostics no doubt spoke loudly about
spiritual generation and divine knowledge (*gnosis*), but John
reminds the beloved brethren that love is more a sign of regeneration and knowledge than talk can ever be. (Cf. comments at
2:3,29). The true Christian is more of a walker than a talker.
The language of spiritual generation and divine *gnosis* is not
rejected, but love is the distinctive word in the Christian vocabulary. This is why the term "beloved" is so basic (2:7; 3:2,21;
4:1,11).

The negative statement follows the positive (4:8). It is not
possible to know God without love. It may be true that to know
God is to love God, but it is truer to say to love God is to know
God. It is the object of love that is truly known. "But if one
loves God, one is known by him" (I Corinthians 8:3). It will
soon become clear that love focused on God finds the brother
in between, but now God's eternal being as the source of all love
is the theme.

God as love is the second great declaration about God in the
letter. At the beginning "God is light" (1:5) was introduced as
common ground with the Gnostics, but the thought soon moved
into a refutation of their views. Now a distinctive Christian
declaration says "God is love" (4:8). God is more of a definition
of love than love is a definition of God. One can hardly say "love
is God," for love has a variety of meanings. God is the source of
that distinctive love called *agape*. Karl Barth has well said:
"God is He, who in His Son Jesus Christ loves all His children,
in His children all men, and in men His whole creation. God's
being is His loving. He is all that He is as the One who loves.
All His perfections are the perfections of His love."[1]

There is a mother love called *storgē* (natural affection) that
one may learn in infancy as he nurses at his mother's breast.
It is a very important form of love, and he who never learns it
becomes a hard and calloused adult. There is also a brother love
called *philia* (friendship with emotion). This is learned from
playmates in a healthy childhood. It is better to have a little

---

[1] *Church Dogmatics*, III/i, p. 394.

scrapping than go through childhood without it. Then there is the lover's love called *erōs,* sexual love that may bind male and female together until death, or it may be lacking and lead to familiar forms of frustration and alienation. Divine love (*agape*) embraces all of these lower levels of love, but it is more. It is that spontaneous, self-sacrificing love that gives ultimate meaning to all other loves. Charles Wesley was right when he called it "love divine, all loves excelling." "God is love." He is not only the source of love; he is the same as love.

God's love is most completely manifested in his historical action in Jesus Christ (4:9-10). Thus far God's love has been spoken of as if it is manifested in the human lover. This is true in a limited sense, but the full meaning of *agapē* is found in God's self-manifestation in his only Son. God's final manifestation of himself is at the *parousia* (the word associated with the second coming of Christ, 2:28), but there is a past and present manifestation in his Son in the *koinōnia* which manifests the fellowship of love.

God's love in historical action is manifested first in the *sending* of his Son into the godless *kosmos* (4:9). For the seventh time *en toutōi* (by this) introduces a descriptive statement (2:3,5; 3:10,16,19; 4:2,9,10,13,17). This is still love manifested "in us" (*en hēmin*). A. T. Robertson is careful to point out that the Greek phrase means "in us," not "among us" nor "to us" (cf. 4:12). God's love was of course manifested in an objective way in Jesus Christ, but the emphasis here is on personal experience of the historical event.

God's sending of his Son was the objective event in history. That was denied by the Gnostics. They could believe that God sent his Son to dwell in Jesus after his baptism and until just before his death, but the idea that God's Son was Jesus in all the days of his flesh, including his death on the cross, was beyond their belief. John is very emphatic to say that God sent his *only* Son into the godless *kosmos* alienated from God and hostile toward God. Son has reference to Jesus alone in John. Believers are called God's little children, young children, and simply children, but never does John call them sons. Son is reserved for Jesus, and here Jesus is called God's only Son. The Greek *monogenēs* is from *monos* (only) *genos* (kind) and means the only one of his kind, unique.[2] *The Revised Standard Version, Today's English Version,* and *The Jerusalem Bible* all agree.

God sent his only Son into the godless *kosmos* to overcome darkness, death, and hate. Overcoming this *kosmos* is the theme of three sections (2:12-17; 4:1-6; 5:1-13). Life was the main theme in part two (2:28-4:6). The giving of life to those in the godless *kosmos* in which death dwells was the purpose for God's sending his Son. The eternal life of God is mediated to his begotten children through his eternal Son. (Cf. John 3:16).

After God sent his Son into the world, he sacrificed him for the sins of the world (4:10). For the eighth time *en toutōi* (by this) is used as a descriptive phrase (cf. 4:9). *Agape* is God's movement toward his children before it is God's children confessing the Father. Plato had much to say about *erōs,* which measured love by the worth of the object. One loved most the most worthy, and the worthless was not to be loved at all. God, however, loved the ungodly in their weakness, sin, and hostility toward him (cf. Romans 5:6,8,10).

The sacrifice of God's Son was a means by which sin was removed. The Greek word is *hilasmos,* a word used earlier in the first section on avoiding sin (2:2). The same phrase "expiation concerning our sins" is used here. The preposition *peri* (concerning) is the most general way to designate the relation between the death of Christ and human sin, but it does not deny the vicarious meaning of Christ's death expressed by *hyper* (on behalf of) and the less frequent substitutionary idea expressed by *anti* (in the place of).

The address of "beloved" is used for the last time as it brings this subsection to a close by ethical application. There is no doubt about God's love being manifested in his historical action by which he sent and sacrificed his only Son, so the word usually translated "if" is rendered "since." The sacrifice of Christ is the solid foundation for Christian action as it is the supreme moment in God's historical action.

The obligation to love one another uses the same word noted in the first section on keeping the commandments where the model by which the Christian is to conduct his life is the historical Jesus

---

[2] See my article on "Only Begotten," *The Interpreter's Dictionary of the Bible.*

(2:6). There is really no difference between an ethic based on the life of Jesus and one based on his death, for both his life and his death were a sacrifice of self-giving love. Loving one another has already been declared as "the message which you heard from the beginning" (3:11). The message and the moral code are one.

The fatal flaw in Protestant Liberalism was the separation of ethics from historical revelation. G. E. Lessing laid the foundations for much of nineteenth century Liberalism in his book called *The Testament of John*. This was based on a story of Jerome about the Apostle John, who, when unable to speak at length in the church, would repeat, "Little children, love one another." When his disciples became tired of hearing always the same thing, they said: "Master, why do you always say this?" Thereupon John gave the answer: "Because this is the commandment of the Lord, and if it is observed then it is enough." This is a beautiful story, and, in a time of rationalistic dogmatism, it is not difficult to see why Lessing wanted to separate morality from dogma, but his humanitarianism fell far short of the testament of John. Historical revelation is the very foundation of moral obligation for John .

(2) Abiding love (4:12-16).

12 No one has ever seen God;
    if we keep on loving one another, God keeps on abiding in us
      and his love is perfected in us.

13 By this we know we abide in him and he in us,
    (because he has given us of his Spirit.

14 And we have seen and we are testifying
    that the Father has sent his Son as the Saviour of the
      godless world.

15 Whoever confesses that Jesus is the Son of God,
    God abides in him, and he in God.

16 And we have known and have believed the love
    which God has in us.)

God is love,
    and whoever abides in love abides in God,
      and God abides in him.

The first four and the last three lines have been assigned to an older source by J. C. O'Neill, but the passage has indeed been "christologically enriched." As the passage now stands, there is an introduction on the vision of God with a parallel on love as abiding and perfect followed by a pattern of trinitarian thought.

The vision of God is a theme both of the Bible and Plato, but the views expressed are very different. For Plato contemplation of Beauty could lead to direct vision of the absolute here and now. The Old Testament writers spoke in terms of hearing the word of the Lord rather than seeing the Lord. Direct vision of God was for the prophets a dangerous thing for sinful men (Isaiah 6:5. Cf. Exodus 33:20).

The teachings of the New Testament follow this view of the Old Testament. When Jesus spoke of seeing God, he put it in the coming age of glory (Matthew 5:8). In this present age his disciples are called to "hear the word of God and keep it" (Luke 11:28). Paul also put direct vision in the future (I Corinthians 13:12). Johannine theology is mystical, but only in the mediated sense. The Gospel says: "No one has ever seen God; the only Son, who is in the bosom of the Father, he has made him known" (1:18). The glory of God is reflected in his Son (1:14) to such a degree that one sees the Father in the Son (14:9), but direct vision of God belongs to the life to come (17:24). This is the meaning of the words: "No one has ever seen God."

Mysticism in church history at times followed the Bible and at other times Plato. The Council of Vienne (1311) resisted the claims of the Beghards and Beguines with the claim that since the Beatific Vision was beyond the natural capacity of man, it could be made accessible only as a gift from God. Benedict XII (1336), however, said the Divine Essence could be seen by direct intuition and face to face with God. Some theologians have taught that direct vision is possible under exceptional circumstances, but this is not the view of John. He is very emphatic: "No one has ever seen God."

This does not mean that God is inaccessible to man. Obedience to the new commandment of love enjoys God's abiding love as a form of true knowledge. Disobedience to God's commandments cuts one off from truth, for loving is knowing and knowing is loving (cf. 2:4-6). God's abiding love is first elaborated in the trinitarian pattern noted already (3:19-24), but the order is in the reverse: Spirit, Son, God.

God's Spirit gives assurance of God's abiding presence (4:13). The characteristic *en toutōi* (by this) describes this mutual indwelling of man in God and God in man. The phrase *en hēmin* (in us) has a special meaning in this section (cf. 4:9,12,13,16), and it seems always to point toward this God-mysticism. It was introduced in the previous passage in the trinitarian pattern where it was also related to the Spirit (3:24), but the discussion on many types of spirits delayed further statement. In the first reference to the Spirit the aorist tense, punctiliar action, was used, but now the perfect tense serves to point out the permanence of God's gift. The witness of the Spirit to the historical Jesus comes later (5:7).

This mutual indwelling of God and man is seen also in the Christ-mysticism of Paul. The sending of God's Son to be born of a woman is followed by the sending of his Spirit into the hearts of his adopted sons (Galatians 4:4-6). Real assurance springs out of the witness of God's Spirit with man's spirit (Romans 8:15-16). The God-mysticism of John and the Christ-mysticism of Paul are much the same, and the neglect of this abiding fellowship with God has often left the church a desert without an oasis. In reaction against the unmediated mysticism of the Platonic tradition there has been a neglect of the mediated mysticism of the New Testament.

God's Son is the mediator of this true mysticism (4:14-15). This has two aspects: God's sending and man's confessing. The prologue of I John confronts the godless *kosmos* and the godly *koinōnia* with this supreme moment of human history (1:1-4). That which is seen is the tent of God in which his glory has come to dwell (John 1:14). In the signs and in the sayings of Jesus, God's sending becomes the preparation for his sacrifice to remove human sin.

The term "Savior of the *kosmos*" shocks. The *kosmos* is the godless mass of humanity estranged and hostile to God. God's children are told not to love that which is in this godless *kosmos* (2:15-17), yet the Son of God is called its Savior. The same voice is heard in the Gospel of John. God loved the *kosmos* so much that his Son was sent to save it rather than to condemn it (3:16-21). The despised Samaritans are the ones who proclaim Jesus to be "the Savior of the *kosmos*" (4:42), and this is the only other place in the Johannine writings where this term is used of the Son of God. The idea, however, is truly Johannine (cf. 2:1-2).

The confessing of the Son has already been noted in John's great confession (2:22-23). This confession is the criterion that distinguishes the true prophets from the false (4:2f), and here it is the sign of the mutual indwelling of God and man (4:15). Any claim to mystical union with God that omits the mediation of God's Son is to be rejected, and this was the Gnostic heresy.

God's giving of his spirit and God's sending of his Son open the way for God himself to abide in his children. Knowledge of God and generation by God are not rejected as valid experience, but love is the sign that they are real. Knowing and believing are knowledge and belief about God's love. A great confession of Jesus as "the Holy One of God" in the Gospel of John uses the same verbs in the same perfect tense, but in reverse order (6:69).

The declaration that "God is love" is repeated (4:8,16), but this time the positive experience of abiding love has taken the place of the negative statement about knowledge. The constant emphasis on the mutual indwelling of God the lover and man the beloved is the true meaning of abiding love. C. H. Dodd has well said: "The passage is the high-water mark of the thought of the epistle." Amos N. Wilder adds: "The greatest themes of the epistle are focused in this verse." With them many would agree.

(3) Perfect love (4:17-18).

17 By this has love been perfected with us,
     that we may have confidence in the Day of Judgment;

because as that One is [in the love of the Father]
     we are also in this godless world.

18 There is no fear in love,
     but perfect love casts out fear;
   because fear has to do with punishment,
     and he who fears has not been perfected in love.

The demonstrative phrase "by this" (en toutōi) appeared twice in the comment about manifested love (4:9-10), once in reference to abiding love (4:13), and now it is used to resume the discussion on perfect love (4:12,17). The *en hēmin* (in us) has become *meth' hēmōn* (with us), but the meaning is much the same as saying "God loved us" (4:11) and "the love God has in us" (4-16). It is the love of God fully developed in the human situation and in spiritual experience.

The fruit of this perfect love is stated as the possession of confidence (4:17) and the absence of fear (4:18). Confidence may be a present possession in prayer (3:21; 5:14) or a preparation for the *parousia* (2:28, 4:17). The Day of the Judgment (literally translated) is at the *parousia* of God in which the Son of God with God's children will be manifested in glory and the secrets of men's hearts will be made known (cf. I Corinthians 4:1-5; II Corinthians 5:10). The concept of a present judgment (*krisis*) is in Johannine theology (John 3:19), but the Day of the Judgment is future (John 5:22,27).

The "that One" is clearly Jesus in Johannine theology (2:6; 3:3,5,7,16; 4:17; John 7:11; 9:12,28; 19:21). Rudolf Bultmann has added the explanatory word *en tēi agapēi tou patros* (in the love of the Father) on the conjecture that the text has been altered. In any case it is true to the meaning of the passage. Confidence in perfect love is abiding in the Father's love as Jesus the Son of God did during all the days of his flesh (John 15:9-10; 17:20-23). As God worked through the Son, the embodiment of perfect love, so now he works in his children as they are perfected in love (cf. John 5:20; 14:10). The mutual indwelling of the Father and the Son has become the mutual indwelling of the Father and the children.

The imitation of Jesus in this godless *kosmos* has appeared several times in I John. God's children are to live as he lived (2:6; 3:3) and love as he loved (3:16; 4:17). It can hardly be said that conflict exists between the example of the historical Jesus and the theology about the eternal Son. Eternal Son and historical Jesus are united in the incarnation as example and expiation are united in his death. The either/or mentality of nineteenth century Liberalism and twentieth century Fundamentalism would seem strange to John. As there was a mission for the Son in the godless *kosmos,* so there is a mission for the apostles and all future disciples (John 17).

Love and confidence are followed by a comparison of love and fear (4:18). As perfect love and confidence are never separated, so perfect love and fear can never be united. Fear appears three times as a noun and once as a participle in four lines. The presence of fear is the absence of love, and the absence of love is the eclipse of God in human experience. Nicholas Berdyaev, the great Russian prophet who lived most of his life in exile, had good reason to say:

> Man kills from fear; at the root of every murder, whether committed by an individual person or by a state, lies fear and slavery. Fear and slavery always have hateful results. If man were to succeed in triumphing over slavish fear, he would cease to murder. From fear of death man sows death, as the result of feeling a slave, he desires to dominate. Domination is always constrained to kill. The state is always subject to fear and therefore it is constrained to kill. It has no desire to wrestle against death. Men in authority are very much like gangsters.[3]

Perfect love sets man free from the deadly cycle of fear—hate—murder—death.

The incompatibility of perfect love and fear is brought out by the strong verb "casts out" (exō ballei). Jesus will not cast out those who come to him (John 6:37), but the blind man who believed was cast out of the synagogue in Jerusalem (9:34-35). Jesus will cast out the Devil, the ruler of this godless kosmos (12:31), and the branch that bears no fruit is cast forth from the vine (15:6). Love and fear are two of the most powerful emotions in life, but love is stronger. As Jesus the Stronger One cast out Satan and the demons (Mark 3:22-27), so perfect love casts out fear.

Fear has to do with punishment. One fears the anticipated punishment for his sins. The word for punishment is kolasis, used in the New Testament only here and in Matthew 25:46. It is derived from the verb kolazo which means to be lopped off as a fruitless branch is lopped off a vine. The Gospel of Matthew uses the word as a synonym for being cut to pieces (cf. Matthew 24:51; 25:46). Fear anticipates being cut off from God at the Day of Judgment. It is much the same as Paul's statement about

---

[3] *Slavery and Freedom* (New York: Charles Scribner's Sons, 1944), p. 251.

the spirit of slavery (Romans 8:15). The general meaning of fear may be seen in the phrase "fear of the Jews" (John 7:13; 19:28; 20:19).

A. T. Robertson compares three Greek words for punishment. *"Timōria* has only the idea of penality, *kolasis* has also that of discipline, while *paideia* has that of chastisement (Hebrews 12:7)." He also adds the Latin of Bengel's famous description of four types of men: "without fear and love; with fear without love; with fear and love; without fear with love." The fourth is the true man. That is why the late Franklin D. Roosevelt voiced the universal hope of humanity when he coined the phrase "freedom from fear."

(4) Brotherly love (4:19-21).

19 We love, because he first loved us.
20 If anyone says, "I love God,"
     and hates his brother, he is a liar;
   for whoever does not love his brother whom he has seen,
     cannot love God whom he has not seen.
21 And this commandment we have had from him,
     that whoever loves God should love his brother also.

The declaration about the priority of God's love resumes the demonstration of love (4:10,19). God's prior love was manifested in the sending and the sacrifice of his Son concerning our sins (4:9-10). This is a general statement about love for God and man. The *Authorized (King James) Version* adds "him" to "we love," but this "him" is missing in many of the best manuscripts. There is no object expressed as in 3:18. The priority of God's love is necessary for us to love either God or man. The two, as the next three parallels indicate, can never be separated in any case.

The first parallel is a refutation that puts love and hate in contrast (4:20a). Quoting an opponent for refutation has been the method used in reference to both fellowship with God and knowledge of God (1;6,8,10; 2:4), and it is used of love for God. Hatred for a brother is hatred for God's child, and this is a contradiction (2:9-10; 3:11-17; 5:1). Anyone who says he can love God and hate his brother is a liar. It may sound blunt to call the hater a liar, but John uses the word freely. Those who say they have not sinned make God a liar (1:10), and he who claims he

knows God while he is disobedient to his commandments is a liar
(2:4). Hating a brother is hating what God loves, and this con-
tradicts truth.

The explanation of this contradiction follows in the next parallel
(4:20b). The brother is the visible image of God. Loving God
means loving his image. This belief belongs to New Testament
wisdom, for James exposed this absurdity. With the same tongue
the double-minded man attempts to bless the Lord and Father
and at the same time he curses men made in God's likeness (3:9).
For John, God will not be seen as he is until the *parousia* (3:2).
He has never been seen by man (4:12; John 1:18). The only way
to make God an object of love is to love the brother whom
God loves.

The application of brotherly love is obedience to the new commandment (4:21). This has been the theme of two other sections
(2:3-11; 3:10b-24), but it has now been brought to a grand climax.
This is the sixth of the great declarations in I John (1:5; 2:25;
3:1,23; 4:3,21; 5:3,4,6,9,11,14,20). The giver of the new commandment is not clear in this parallel. *The Centenary Translation* says
we have it from God and *Today's English Version* says we have
it from Christ. In both the Synoptic Gospels (Mark 12:28-34;
Matthew 22:24-40; Luke 10:25-28) and the Gospel of John, Jesus
gives the commandment to love (13:34; 15:12), but God seems
always to be the commander in I John (2:4-5; 3:22-24; 5:2-3),
and this runs through the whole of this section on keeping the
commandment (4:7-21). It makes little difference in meaning,
but God is the subject in this section. Keeping God's commandment of love is the ground of Christian assurance.

Brotherly love was a distinctive of the early Christians. The
Emperor Julian, called the apostate, in a letter to Arsacius, the
pagan high priest of Galatia, declared that the power of the
Christians to lead people away from the pagan gods was due to
the brotherly love which Christians manifested along with the
thoughtful manner in which they cared for their dead and the
holiness of their lives.[4] Brotherly love has not lost is power, and
it is still the most potent weapon of Christians who dare to put
it into practice.

---

[4] *The Works of the Emperor Julian,* Epistle 49 (New York: G. P. Putnam, 1923), Vol.
III, p. 69.

2. Overcoming the godless *kosmos* (5:1-13): faith.
   (1) The triumph of God's children (5:1-5).

1 Everyone who believes that Jesus is the Christ has been
     begotten of God,
               and everyone who loves the begetter loves him who
               has been begotten of him.

2 By this we know that we love the children of God,
     when we love God and do his commandments.

3 For this is love for God,
     that we keep his commandments:

4 and his commandments are not burdensome,
     because everything begotten of God overcomes the
          godless world;

   and this is the victory that overcame the godless world,
     our faith.
5   Who is it that overcomes the godless world but he who
           believes that Jesus is the Son of God?

Faith now flows into the river of love in great fullness. The bond
between believing in Jesus Christ and brotherly love has already
been declared as one commandment (3:23). The danger of false
belief (4:1) and the blessing of true belief (4:16) have also
appeared, but this is the first point at which believing has become
a dominant factor. It is now the means by which the Christian
overcomes the godless *kosmos* (5:1,4,5,10,13). Believing has very
definite content, so this section begins and ends with a Christological formulation (5:1,5). These formulations were stated briefly
earlier (2:22-23), but now the bond between the two is
strengthened.

The belief that Jesus is the Christ was denied by the Cerinthian
Gnostics. For them Jesus and Christ were two different persons,
and the Christ came to dwell in Jesus only at his baptism and left
him before his death. This will be refuted in detail in the next
section, but now the relationship between believing and loving
requires a restatement of how love for God requires love for other
Christians. This is done in two steps.

First, love for God means love for God's children (5:1-2). The shift from the metaphor of another Christian as a brother (4:19-21) to that of the child opens the way for a more complete statement of divine generation. Human believing leads to divine begetting. This statement has often been reversed, especially in the tradition of Calvinism. A. T. Robertson speaks favorably of a statement by Robert Law in his popular book on *The Tests of Life* which says: "The Divine begetting is the antecedent not the consequent of believing." This opens the door to double predestination in which God is said first to regenerate those who are to believe. This surely is not the order in the Gospel of John (1:12-13; 3:16).

The words about the begetter and the begotten have the marks of a proverb. God is the parent who begets and the Christian is the child who is begotten, but God begets those who first believe. The idea of believers being begotten of God appears frequently in I John (2:29; 3:9; 4:7; 5:4,18); and this explains in part why believers are so often called little children (*teknia*, 2:12,28; 3:7,18; 4:4; 5:21), young children (*paidia*, 2:14,18) or just children (*tekna*, 3:1,10; 5:2). Even the ideas of the brother (2:9,11; 3:11-17; 4:21) and the beloved (3:2,21; 4:1,7,11) are based on this begetting. At this point the idea of brotherhood has flowered into a whole family of God in which all Christians are related to one another as brothers and to God as children. Being begotten and brotherly love are beautifully blended.

That which has been said in terms of begetting is now restated in terms of loving (5:2). By this (*en toutōi*) has become a commonplace (2:3,5; 3:10,16,19; 4:2,9,13,17; 5:2). C. H. Dodd is surprised that John has shifted from love for man as "the immediate *datum* of experience" to love for God. The usual order is love for God by love for man (3:15; 5:20), but it is not correct to alter the order of words as Dodd suggests. Love for the begetter led to love for the begotten, and now love for God leading to love for God's children is only a restatement. Love for the father means love for his child, so love for God means love for his children. Obedience to God means *doing* his commandments, not *keeping*, as in the *Authorized (King James) Version*, and he commands us to love his children. Doing his commandments is like doing the truth (1:6). Dodd has overlooked the fact that the same was said in the previous section in terms of loving the brother (4:21). Love is a perfect circle that runs both ways.

This leads to the second step in which love for God is keeping his commandments (5:3-4a). The shift from the singular (commandment, 4:21) to the plural (commandments, 5:2-3) has been once in the reverse order (4:3-4,7-8) and once both ways (3:22-24). Love is now formulated as a law (5:3), but it is a law that is not so burdensome as was the law of Moses (5:4. Cf. Matthew 23:4). This is the seventh of the thirteen great declarations in I John (1:5; 2:25; 3:11,23; 4:3,21; 5:3,4,6,9,11,14,20).

Love as a law is formulated at every stage of New Testament teaching. It is the higher righteousness or the new *torah* in the teaching of Jesus (Matthew 5:20), "the perfect law, the law of liberty" in James (1:25), "the law of Christ" in Paul (Galatians 6:2), and "the new commandment" in John (2:3-4,7-8; II John 6; John 13:34; 14:15,21). Keeping the commandments is living according to this new law of love (2:3-11; 3:11-24; 4:7-21).

Love as a law is light (5:4). "Love for God lightens the demands" (A. T. Robertson). This makes it different from all other laws that increase self-centered anxiety. This is the gentle yoke of Jesus described in his immortal words of invitation to the weary (Matthew 11:28-30).

> Come to me all who labor and are heavy laden, and I will give you rest,
> Take my yoke upon you, and learn of me;
> for I am gentle and lowly in heart, and you will find rest for your souls.
> For my yoke is easy, and my burden light.

God's generation in his children makes it possible for them to love him and one another and thus overcome the ways of the godless *kosmos* where people live according to "the lusts of the flesh and the lust of the eyes and the vainglory of life" (2:16). God's word (*logos*) gives strength to young men to overcome the Evil One and the godless *kosmos* in his embrace (2:14; 5:9). God's seed (*sperma*) makes it impossible for his children to continue in the life of sin (3:9). God in his children is greater than all the power of the Evil One in the *kosmos* (4:4). These are some of the variations on the victory of God's children over the

godless *kosmos* of unredeemed humanity. The Son of God overcame the *kosmos* by his passion, and now God's children have
power to overcome (John 16:33).

The last couplet (5:4b,5) is at times grouped with the next
section, but it is really a summary on the triumph of God's
children (cf. Romans 8:37). This eighth of the great declarations
in I John has also the marks of a proverb. It is impossible to
reproduce all the play on sound and words in the Greek declaration
hautē estin hē nikē hē nikēsasa, but William Barclay's "this is the
conquest which has conquered" comes close. It has all the ring
of a decisive battle in which God's children have come to the
point of believing in the Son of God and God has begotten them
as his children. This is "our faith," the only time in the Letters of
John and in the Gospel of John that the noun for belief is used.
Our faith is our triumph. To believe (3:23; 4:1,16) and to confess
(2:23; 4:2-3,15) have much the same meaning.

The formulation of faith in a Christological definition may be
called an echo of the great confession of I John (2:22-23). The
first echo was heard in the third section on keeping the commandment (4:15). This is aimed at the Gnostic heresy that refused
to identify Jesus with the Son of God. Some ancient authorities
have a baptismal confessional similar to this at Acts 8:37. There
is no doubt that an anti-Gnostic confession is intended.

(2) The testimony of God (5:6-13).

6 This is he who came through water and blood, Jesus Christ;
　　not by the water only but by the water and by the blood.

7 And the Spirit is the witness,
　　because the Spirit is the truth.

8 (Because there are three that bear witness,
　　the Spirit, and the water, and the blood,
　　　and the three agree in one.

9 If we receive the testimony of men,
　　the testimony of God is greater;
　　for this is the testimony of God,
　　　because he has borne witness concerning his Son.)

10 Whosoever believes in the Son of God has the testimony in
himself,
Whoever does not believe God has made him a liar,
because he has not believed in the testimony that God
has borne concerning his Son.

11 And this is the testimony:
that God gave us eternal life,
and this life is in his Son;

12 Whoever has the Son has life,
whoever does not have the Son of God does not have life.

13 These things I wrote to you that you may know that you have
eternal life,
to you who go on believing in the name of the
Son of God.

God's testimony on behalf of his Son, Jesus Christ, is developed
in three steps: the external testimony of the Spirit to the historical
Jesus (5:6-7), the internal testimony in the believer himself (5:10),
and the content of the testimony (5:11-12). In a general way
there is a trinitarian pattern of Spirit-God-Son (cf. 3:19-24; 4:13-
16), but this has been combined with a spurious passage (5:7)
in the *Authorized (King James) Version,* a genuine Johannine
comment (5:8-9), and what appears to be an older conclusion to
the letter (5:13). It has often been said that this is at once the
most difficult passage of the letter, both in terms of text and
theology, and one of the most important for understanding its
purpose.

The external testimony is rooted in the historical Jesus. His
coming "through water and blood" is one of the great declarations
in the present form of the letter (1:5; 2:25; 3:11,23; 4:3,21; 5:3,
4,6,9,11,20). His coming *di' hydatos* (through water) has reference
to the baptism of Jesus by John the Baptist (Mark 1:9-11; Matthew
3:16-17; Luke 3:21-22). At that time God gave his testimony
by anointing Jesus with the Spirit (cf. Acts 10:38). John interprets this in terms of historical testimony to an eternal reality, not
as the occasion when God adopted Jesus as his Son. Jesus is
for him the eternal Son of God who was sent into the world,

from the point of view of God, and came into the world from the point of view of man.

The "not by water only" implies that there were those who taught that Jesus became the Son of God at his baptism and ceased to be the Son of God before the shedding of his blood at his crucifixion. Irenaeus of Lyons told how a form of Gnostic Judaism said that Christ descended upon Jesus at his baptism and flew back to the Unknown Father before the crucifixion, "leaving Jesus, and Jesus suffered and rose again, but Christ remained impassible, being by nature spiritual" (*Against Heresies*, I.XXVI.1,2). It is that heresy associated with the name of Cerinthus of Ephesus that John is refuting. Jesus was the Son of God, the Christ, both at his baptism and his crucifixion.

The idea of a witness is a very important concept in John (John 1:7,15; 4:39; 5:31,36f; 19:35). At one place, the baptism, God bore witness by the Spirit. This is so important that the Gospel of John does not even mention the baptism of Jesus with water (1:32-34). After the crucifixion Jesus said that the Paraclete as "the Spirit of truth" would bear witness of him (15:26). The "truth" in I John 5:7 is an echo of "the Spirit of truth" in the Gospel of John (14:17; 15:26). This is another link between the Johannine writings and Qumran.[5]

The *Authorized (King James) Version* has as 5:7 a passage that is missing in most manuscripts. "For there are three that bear record in heaven, the Father, the Word, and the Holy Ghost: and these three are one." Cyprian of Carthage expounded the Trinity, in a most orthodox manner, along these lines, but they were first cited by Instantius, a disciple of a Spanish heretic name Priscillian who died in A.D. 385. Priscillianism, a form of Manichean dualism, was condemned at the Council of Braga in 563. Priscillian was a Spanish heretic of the fourth century who taught an ascetic system of doctrine that made a radical distinction between the soul and the body. Manes or Mani, from whom the term Manichaeanism comes, was a Persian of the third century who taught the same type of dualism found in Priscillian, but he put special emphasis on the dualism between the kingdom of light to which the soul belongs and the kingdom of darkness to which the body belongs.

---

[5] Otto Betz, *Der Paraklet* (Leiden/Köln: E. J. Brill, 1963), pp. 110-149.

These were rejected by orthodox Christians who saw in such thought a threat to the doctrines of creation, incarnation, and the resurrection of the body.

Despite the condemnation of Priscillianism and the absence of this passage from the great manuscripts, the great fathers of the church, and Jerome's Latin Vulgate, Erasmus created a stir by omitting it from his first Greek Testament edited in 1516. No Latin manuscript before A.D. 800 had the passage, and these are of African or Spanish origin. Four late Greek codices have the words translated from the Latin. The Latin Vulgate of 1514, the so-called Sixto-Clementine edition, included the spurious words, so the typical heresy hunters denounced the great humanist. Erasmus, in a compromising mood, promised to put it in the next edition if it could be found in any Greek manuscript. Unfortunately, manuscript no. 34, now in Trinity College, Dublin, was presented to him, so true to his word he put it in the 1522 edition. Stephanus included it in his *Textus Receptus* of 1550. From this background it got into the *Authorized (King James) Version*.

As late as 1897, the Holy Office in Rome declared the text authentic, but on June 2, 1927, they were forced to reverse the pronouncement. No modern Roman Catholic scholar defends the passage. The great commentary by Rudolf Schnackenburg, a Roman Catholic authority on the Johannine Writings, has all the details on the problem, and *The Jerusalem Bible* and *The Jerome Biblical Commentary*, splendid Bible helps by Roman Catholic scholars, do not accept the passage as authentic. This should be a solemn warning to those who would settle the questions of historical research by hasty pronouncements.

The Johannine comment of verses 8-9, unlike the so-called Johannine comma of 5:7, is genuine. This parenthetical comment is a mystical meditation on the water and the blood. Water and blood now mean more than the baptism and the crucifixion of Jesus. As the believer is baptized in the name of Jesus and receives communion blessed in his name, the water and the blood are added to the Spirit to make three witnesses. This reflects the Hebrew idea of three witnesses to make valid testimony (Deuteronomy 19:15), but the meaning is spiritual. The one witness of 5:7 has been expanded to three, but there is a oneness in the threeness: "the three agree in one" (5:8). The shift from the literary form of the doublet to that of the triplet supports the suggestion that 5:8-9 is a parenthesis.

The main argument of God's testimony to Jesus Christ is resumed by the statement on the internal testimony (5:10). The testimony of history is now one the believer has within himself. This supplements the external testimony of history, but it does not supplant it. Faith unites the external testimony of history with the internal testimony of the heart. This is the same as the *chrisma* received from the Holy One which abides in the believer (2:20,27). The Gnostic effort to separate the objective form of the historical Jesus from the subjective experience of mystical knowledge is declared a failure and a denial of the testimony of God. God's testimony comes to the believer in many other historical forms such as John the Baptist, the works of Jesus, and the Old Testament Scripture (John 5:30-40). He who rejects these witnesses does not know the truth and has made God a liar (cf. 2:22-23; 4:1-6).

God's testimony began with the coming of the Son of God into the world (5:6), and the content of that testimony brings the thought back to the Son of God (5:11-12). Eternal life is that content (cf. 1:1-2; 2:25; 3:14-15; 4:9; 5:16,20). Eternal life is first of all a gift (5:11). As God's own life, man can receive it only as an act of God's grace to be received by faith. It is mediated to the believer through Jesus Christ the Son of God (5:12). Jesus as the Son of God has this life in himself (John 5:19-29), but the believer can have it only by mediation (cf. John 3:15-16,36; 10:10; 17:2). Gnostics who deny the Son cut themselves off from the very source of eternal life. Jesus is the life (John 11:25; 14:6).

The Letter concludes much as the Gospel (5:13; John 20:31). Each also has a postscript (5:14-21; John 21). In both, belief in the name of the Son of God, Jesus Christ, brings the certain knowledge that one here and now has eternal life.

3. Avoiding sin (5:14-17): prayer.

14 And this is the confidence that we have in him,
   that if we ask anything according to his will he hears us.

15 And if we know that he hears us in whatever we ask,
   we know that we have the requests which we have asked from
   him.

16 If anyone sees his brother sinning a sin that does not lead to death,

> he should ask, and he will keep on giving him life—to those who sinning does not lead to death.

There is a sin that leads to death—not concerning that am I saying he should ask.

17 All unrighteousness is a sin, and there is a sin that does not lead to death.

Prayer was implicit at the end of the first section on avoiding sin (1:6-2:2), and it became explicit in the second on keeping the commandments (3:21-22). Now prayer is made even more explicit in reference to sin. There is first a general statement on prayer as petition to God (5:14-15).

Confidence in God brings together two characteristic matters already noted (4:15). First of all this is one of the thirteen great declarations in I John (1:5; 2:25; 3:11,23; 4:3,21; 5:3,4,6,9,11,14,20). This declaration again relates prayer to *parrēsia*, the freedom and confidence to speak in God's presence (3:21; 5:14). This freedom is also related to the final judgment at the *parousia* of God (2:28; 4:17). This holy boldness usually has reference to God (II Corinthians 3:12; Hebrews 10:19), but it is also characteristic of the apostolic witness to others (Acts 4:13). It is one of the great words of the New Testament. See 2:28 for the important lecture by W. C. Van Unnik.

The content of this confidence is that God answers requests that are according to his will. "He" and "him" and "his" refer to God when it is not clearly a reference to man. Prayer in its most basic form is asking and receiving, but the first step is finding the will of God. God and his will come before all human requests, as in the model prayer of Jesus (Matthew 6:9-13—Luke 11:2-4). The will of God may lead into the ordeal of suffering and persecution (I Peter 4:19) or even to death as it did for Jesus himself (Mark 14:32-42). Asking may also not result in receiving "because you ask wrongly, to spend it on your passions" (James 4:3). The whole purpose of God is the accomplishment of his will in the apostles and in the church in general (Galatians 1:4; Ephesians 1:5,11).

Conditions for answered prayer have already been stated in terms of keeping God's commandments (3:2), but this is living according to the will of God. Living and praying according to the will of God are prerequisites for petitions to be granted. This is God-centered praying. Christ-centered praying is more characteristic of the Gospel of John, for there praying in the name of Jesus (14:14) and abiding in the word of Jesus (15:7) are prerequisite to answered prayer. For John the two centers are not radically different, for the Father and the Son are inseparable (I John 1:3; 2:23). It is only in a general way that distinction can be made between God-mysticism and Christ-mysticism.

The declaration on prayer is followed by an amplification (5:15). Confidence is now expressed in terms of knowledge ("we know . . . we know"). If we know that he hears, we know that we receive. Knowing that God hears belongs to the great certainties of faith (Matthew 7:7):

> Ask, and it will be given you;
> seek, and you will find;
> knock, and it will be opened to you.

It is the confidence of a little child who knows before he asks that the father will grant his request. The request is then made in loving obedience.

This confidence is in the repetition of "we know." The word "requests" is found only here in John, but Paul uses the word in the same context. "Have no anxiety about anything, but in everything by prayer and supplication with thanksgiving let your requests be made known to God" (Philippians 4:6). The present tense followed by the perfect ("we have the requests which we have asked from him") is indeed what A. T. Robertson called "possession by anticipation." The certainty of the answer makes the request as good as answered. "Therefore, I tell you, whatever you ask in prayer, believe that you receive it and you will" (Mark 11:24).

The general declaration on prayer as petition prepares the way for the more special application to intercessory prayer for sinners (5:16-17). William Barclay says: "There is no doubt that this is a most difficult and a most disturbing passage". Very true, but it is more disturbing to accept than it is difficult to interpret. The key words are rather clear in the letter. A brother, despite Rudolf Bultmann's statement that it at times means fellow-man, seems always to be either a flesh and blood brother or a fellow Christian (2:9-11; 3:10,12-17; 4:20-21; 5:16; III John 3,5,10). Sin (*hamartia*) is used several times, and twice it is defined as lawlessness (*anomia*, 3:4). Lawlessness and unrighteousness (*adikia*) are synonyms. Life (*zoē*) is always eternal life; the very life of God (1:1,2; 2:25; 3:14,15; 5:11-13,16,20). Death (*thanatos*) is used only once in I John outside 5:16-17, but there the meaning of spiritual death is crystal clear (3:14).

Sin that does not lead to spiritual death would then be an act of lawlessness or unrighteousness. Unrighteousness may be cleansed and forgiven (1:7,9). Felowship with God is impossible while one walks in sin (1:5-10), but God's little children may fall into such sin (2:1-2). Lawlessness is no daily practice of those in whom God dwells (3:4-10). Therefore, as a result of intercessory prayer on the part of believers, God will give spiritual life to the brother who had a temporary moral lapse and had broken fellowship. The sap stopped flowing in the branch, but it was not lopped off from the vine (John 15:1-11). Intercessory prayer is a precious jewel (James 5:14; Hebrews 13:8-9; I Thessalonians 5:25; Colossians 4:2-4; Ephesians 6:18-20; I Timothy 4:1).

What now is the sin that leads to spiritual death and deprives one of spiritual life? Is it possible for one to pass from spiritual death to spiritual life and then pass again from spiritual life back into spiritual death? What does John mean by the blunt statement: "There is a sin that leads to death"? This is perhaps a concession to those who were so rigid that they thought every sin by a Christian was deadly, for John's main point is that intercessory prayer will help those whose sin does not lead to death. Nevertheless, there is agreement that: "There is a sin that leads to death." This is the disturbing fact difficult to receive. It would have saved a lot of argument if John had said more!

Old Testament sacrifices were efficacious only for sins done unwittingly (Leviticus 4:2ff.; 5:1ff.; Numbers 15:22ff.). No provision was made for sins done with a "high hand" (Numbers 15:30). Jesus himself spoke of those who blaspheme the Holy Spirit by attributing his works to Satan (Mark 3:28-29; Matthew 12:31-32;

Luke 12:10) and of those who deny him (Mark 8:38; Matthew 10:32-33; Luke 9:26; 12:8-9). Even temporary denial, as in the case of Peter, may be forgiven (Mark 14:66-72; Luke 22:31-32). Hebrews has five long warnings about the dangers of falling away (2:1-4; 3:7—4:13; 6:1-20; 10:19-39; 12:1-29), and Paul fears the Galatians have fallen from grace (1:6; 3:1-5; 4:8-9; 5:1,7; 6:7-10). These warnings and many more are found in the New Testament before the Johannine writings appeared on the scene.

The Gospel of John was rather blunt about Judas Iscariot (6:71; 17:21) and those branches in the vine that bear no fruit (15:2,6). Those who became antichrists have already been noted (2:19), and the remarks there should be read again, especially the statements by A. T. Robertson. William Barclay mentions the lame argument that this is a sin that leads to a punishment of physical death inflicted by man. The infliction of physical death by God upon sinners is mentioned by Paul (I Corinthians 11:30. Cf. Acts 5:1-11), but that would be the loss of *bios* (physical life), not *zoe* (spiritual life). It seems impossible to avoid the conclusion that this is a sin so serious that it cuts one off from eternal life, and believers are not requested to pray for such sinners. The warning against idols (5:21) may be a clue, for Christians in Asia often faced the ordeal by which they were required to make a choice between Caesar and Christ. If they chose Caesar, they worshiped him by burning incense before his bust (cf. Revelation 13:11; 22:11). A moving account of this is *The Martyrdom of Polycarp*, Bishop of Smyrna, who died the martyr's death at the age of eighty-six in A.D. 156.

Two Latin traditions have handicapped the straightforward interpretation of this sin as the renunciation of Christ. One began with Tertullian (c.160-c220) who taught that three post-baptismal sins were unpardonable. Apostasy itself was one, but he added adultery and murder. In the process of time a whole theology of mortal sins developed from the one mortal sin of I John 5:16-17. The second was first formulated by Augustine (354-430), who argued that a gift of perseverance was given to a limited number called the elect. Catholic theology developed the first in great detail, but Calvinism went to seed on the second. Many still do specious exegesis to bring Scripture in line with these distortions of New Testament doctrine, but it seems impossible. The outcome has been that the creeds go one way and the commentaries another. It would be much easier if the creeds were discarded!

4. Guarding against the enemy (5:18-21): knowledge.

> 18 We know that everyone who has been begotten of God does not make a practice of sin,
>> but if one has been begotten of God, God keeps him,
>> and the Evil One does not touch him.

> 19 We know that we are of God
>> and the whole godless world lies in the Evil One.

> 20 (And we know that the Son of God has come
>> and has given us understanding
>>> in order that we may know the True One;

> And we are in the True One, in his Son Jesus Christ.
> This is the True God and Eternal life).

> 21   Little children, keep yourselves from idols.

The argument by J. C. O'Neill for verse 20 being a parenthetical comment makes for two triplets on God and the Evil One (5:18-19,21) and one on the True God (5:20). As the text now stands, there are three great certainties of the Christian life that conclude the letter. Each begins with the "we know" noted twice in verse 15 (cf. 3:2,14). The confidence in prayer has led to certain knowledge on other beliefs.

The first certainty (5:18) begins on the note sounded in 3:9a ("Everyone who is begotten of God does not make a practice of sin"). In 3:9b it was God's *sperma* (seed), interpreted as the *logos*, that kept one from a life of continuous sin. That which keeps him out of the reach of the Evil One is called *ho gennētheis* (literally, the begotten). Who is the begotten? In every other instance in I John, the verb *gennao* has reference to God's children (2:29; 3:9; 4:7; 5:1,14. Cf. John 1:13; 3:3). Seven times it is combined with "of God" and twice with "of him," meaning the same.

The *Authorized (King James) Version* and *The Centenary Trans-*

lation interpret the word to mean a child of God, following the
textual reading which says he "keeps himself" (*tērei heauton*).
The *heauta* (yourselves) in 5:21 has that idea too. The reading
heauton has the support of the great *Codex Sinaiticus,* but most
textual critics follow the reading "keeps him" (*terei auton*) of
Alexandrinus and *Vaticanus.* Most commentaries and translations
interpret this to mean "the Son of God keeps him safe," as in
Today's English Version (Good News for Modern Man). The
real problem with the majority opinion is the use of the verb
gennao with the Son of God. In I John it is the children, not the
Son, who are begotten of God, and the shift from the perfect
participle to the aorist does not alter this fact. The best the great
A. T. Robertson can do is refer to John 18:37 where the "of God"
does not appear.

The begotten seems clearly to mean the begotten child of God,
but how should it be translated and interpreted? If it is a conditional participle, as Bultmann suggests, the subject of *tērei* can be
God, and this has been followed in the above translation. The idea
of God keeping his children agrees with God's *sperma* in 3:9,
and this agrees with the teaching of the Gospel of John. "While
I was with them, I kept them in your name, which you have
given me; I have guarded them, and none of them perished but
the son of perdition, that the scripture must be fulfilled . . . I
do not pray that you should take them out of the *kosmos,* but that
you should keep them from the Evil One" (17:12,15. Cf. 10:27-
29). As the Evil One, the ruler of this *kosmos* has no power over
Christ, so he has no power over the Christian (John 14:30).

The second triplet continues the same line of thought by shifting
from the singular to the plural (5:19,21). The "of God" is now
combined with "we are" (cf. 4:6) to include John and the whole
koinōnia. The whole *kosmos* passively lies in the embrace of the
Evil One. The verb is used of baby Jesus "lying in a manger"
(Luke 2:12). The *kosmos* is the abode of death and the Devil.
Light and darkness, life and death, love and hate make the moral
dualism of John. To lie in the Evil One means much the same
as for the hater to abide in death (3:14). God has his *koinōnia,*
and the Evil One has his *kosmos.* Each must choose which group
he will join. It is impossible to belong to both. The begotten
children belong to God.

The second triplet is interrupted by the comment, itself another triplet (5:20). The section on guarding against the enemy has concentrated on God up to this point, but there is a sharp shift to the Son of God. The perfect tense of the verb ("has come") indicates the decisive act by which the Son of God entered history. Another comment said: "For this reason the Son of God was manifested in order that he might destroy the works of the Devil" (3:8). Jesus said: "I proceeded and came forth from God; I came not of my own accord, but he sent me" (John 8:42).

The Son of God brought understanding (*dianoian*). Paul did not hesitate to speak of a Christian *gnōsis* (knowledge), the word made popular by the Gnostic heresy, and *dianoian* (understanding), although the last word appears in a context of darkness and hostility (Colossians 1:21; Ephesians 2:3; 4:18). John never uses *gnōsis,* and this is the only use of *dianoia.* It, therefore, makes his statement that the Son of God brought *dianoia* more surprising.

The True One seems to be the same as the True God, as *Today's English Version* and *The Jerusalem Bible* are bold to translate. The *Authorized (King James) Version* made Jesus Christ "him that is true" by inserting "even" into the text, and *The New English Bible* found it necessary to supply "since we are" to get that meaning. William Barclay tries to have it both ways by saying "even through His Son Jesus Christ." If insertions are to be made it would seem that "and" would be preferable (cf. 1:3), but the *Revised Standard Version* made no additions and makes good sense.

It is possible to make Jesus Christ "the True God." Bruce Vawter, in *The Jerome Biblical Commentary,* says: "In favor of its referring to the Son, it may be argued that thus I John concludes with an explicit affirmation of the divinity of Christ, who is also identified with eternal life as he was at the beginning (1:2); exactly the same procedure is followed in the Gospel (cf. John 1:4,18; 3:28)." This can be further argued by saying Jesus was "full of grace and truth" (John 1:14) and "the truth" (14:6, Cf. 18:37-38). All of this is attractive, but the context and the text favor the True One and the True God as the Father and not the Son (cf. John 17:3).

The sentence about the True God is the last of thirteen declarations in I John (1:5; 2:25; 3:11,23; 4:3,21; 5:3,4,6,9,11,14,20). This is the second time eternal life has been added (2:25; 5:20). A dozen times I John uses this word, seven times in this chapter alone (1:2, 2:25; 3:14,15; 5:11-13,16,20). As always it means participation in the very life of God, the life that comes out of eternity. Participation in this life is possible because of the mediation of Christ (5:11-13). "And this is eternal life, that they may know you, the Only True God, and Jesus Christ, whom you sent" (John 17:3). The Gospel and the First Letter of John say the same. Both had the same purpose (I John 5:13; John 20:31).

The last verse in the letter completes the triplet of verse 19. The begotten are the little children who have their source and origin in God, but they are confronted by the godless *kosmos* that lies in the Evil One. They must ever be on guard at this boundary between God and the Devil. Idols are the symbols of this godless *kosmos* that belongs to the Devil. God-substitutes, as C. H. Dodd calls the idols, are on every hand.

The idols, however, were perhaps more concrete than the Platonic unreality mentioned by Dodd. *The Testament of the Twelve Patriarchs* warns of women and money (*Reuben* 4, *Judah* 19), but more is meant in I John. Diana and perhaps Domitian were their danger. William Barclay is no doubt correct in seeing women and money as a part of pagan worship in the Temple of Diana where fornication and commercialized superstition were big business. In the tenth decade Domitian demanded Emperor worship in Ephesus. After he was officially condemned in A.D. 96, his head was thrown from the temple erected in his honor by the Province of Asia. The head and arm of Domitian's image may be seen today in the Izmir Museum.

I John ends with a jolt, but it is a jolt which pointed toward the future ordeals of Christians in Roman Asia. The great Polycarp was not the first to confront the decision between God and the Evil One. He was one "who put an end to the persecution by sealing, so to speak, through his own witness" (*The Martyrdom of Polycarp* 1:1). There is need for this witness in the modern world which also "lies in the Evil One."

Chapter 6

COMMENTARY ON THE SECOND LETTER OF JOHN

SALUTATION (1-3)

1 The elder to the elect lady and her children,
   whom I love in the truth,
   and not only I but also all who know the truth,

2 because of the truth which abides in us
   and will be with us forever.

3 Grace, mercy, and peace will be with us,
   from God the Father
   and from Jesus Christ the Father's Son,
   in truth and love.

In the usual style of ancient Greek letters, the sender is mentioned first. He calls himself "the elder" (cf. III John 1), a term that may mean no more than an older man held in respect by the readers, but the tone of the letter implies an authority that age alone does not give. Local churches in New Testament times, following the synagogue structure, had pastor-teachers who were called elders (Acts 14:23; I Timothy 5:17; I Peter 5:1), but their authority did not reach beyond the congregation where they served. This elder exercised authority over more than one congregation, a function that gave rise

117

to bishops and archbishops (cf. I Timothy 3:1; 4:14; 5:17-22).

This elder was almost certainly a notable figure in the Ephesian area by the name of John (cf. Revelation 1:4, 9), but here certainty ends. Irenaeus, the Bishop of Lyons toward the end of the second century, came from Asia, and he spoke of the John who wrote the fourth Gospel as "the disciple of the Lord, who also leaned on his breast" (*Against Heresies,* III.1; H.E. V.8). By the year 500 the beloved disciple had been identified with the apostle John and assigned the authorship of all five Johannine writings.

This was not the only tradition. Long before the modern debate on date and authorship there were those who for various reasons raised questions. Origen said some questioned the genuineness of II and III John and assigned them to a John to be distinguished from the Apostle (*Church History,* VI.25.10). Eusebius (c.260-c.340), the Bishop of Caesarea, reported about 325 the view of Papias (c.60-130), the Bishop of Hierapolis and companion of Polycarp of Smyrna, and the report identified "the holy apostles" with "the elders." Eusebius, however, challenged this conclusion and claimed that "two persons in Asia have borne the same name, and that there were two tombs at Ephesus, each of which is still to this day said to be John's" (*Church History* III.39.6). John the Evangelist, he thought, wrote the fourth Gospel, but John the Elder wrote the Revelation. It must be remembered that Eusebius had a strong dislike for the chiliasm of Revelation which Papias promoted. Jerome reports the story of the two tombs and says II and III John are the work of a John the Elder, but he is reserved in his judgment.

The distinction between John the Evangelist and John the Elder is almost universal in modern commentaries, but it hangs on the precipice of prejudice created by the anti-chiliastic attitude of Origen and Eusebius. It is altogether possible that John the Evangelist was the same as John the Elder, and that the tradition of the apostolic origin of all five of the Johannine writings reaching back to Irenaeus is correct. When the writings are read in the order of Revelation, the Letters, the Gospel in its present form, there is little for which chronological development and the style of secretaries cannot account. As Paul used at times Timothy and then Tertius (Romans 16:22), and Peter was reported by John Mark in the Gospel and Silvanus in I Peter (5:12), so the aged apostle John, "the elder" in more than one sense, is reported by more than one secretary.

The recipients of the letter pose another problem. Who is "the elect lady" and who are "her children"? It is hardly worth mentioning the legend about the Virgin Mary and her cult centered about Mary's House at Ephesus, but the tourist will hear the story at the top of the hill. This is based on John 19:26-27 and supported by later mysticism. In another view J. Rendel Harris let his genius get out of control by understanding the phrase *eklektē kyria* to mean "my dear Electa" and called the lady a Gentile proselyte widow of the tribe of Ruth. Verse 13 puts an end to this argument, for it requires a sister with the same name! More can be said for the translation "the elect kyria," but it is doubtful that a woman with such children was loved by so large a circle.

A clue to the meaning may be found in I Peter 5:13 where the church in Babylon (Rome) is spoken of with the feminine *syneklektē* (she who is likewise chosen). Both Israel in the Old Testament (Isaiah 54:5) and the church in the New Testament (Ephesians 5:31-32) are described as women, but it is hardly correct to call this church the Bride of Christ, as Clement of Alexandria thought. This would require two brides, for there are two sisters, so it must be one of the local churches in the Johannine circle of Asia. A letter from the elder of one local church to the members of another local church helps to explain the use of both the singular (4-5,13) and the plural (6,8,10,12). The recipient could be any one of a number of churches other than Ephesus from which the elder probably sent his letter.

The elect lady and her children are especially devoted to the truth, a term used five times in the first four verses (cf. John 8:32). As the Greek word suggests, that which is no longer hidden has been disclosed in the flesh of Jesus Christ. Those of the truth believe in the incarnation of the Son of God over against the Gnostic lie that reduced the historical Jesus to a ghost without flesh and blood. Truth is a technical term for Christian doctrine (cf. John 14:15-16; II Timothy 2:15). Papias called it "the Truth itself" (*Church History* III.39.3).

This truth is both present and future. It is one of those ways to express God's abiding presence in his children (cf. I John 2:6,10,14, 17,19,24,27,28; 3:6,9,14,15,17,24; 4:12,13,15,16). This is not a mysticism that destroys the distinction between God and man, and it could well be called Menism, from the Greek *menein,* to abide, for God abides with his own even into eternity. Truth reaches into eternity because it came out of eternity.

The future tense of the presence leads to the greeting which is a prayer in the form of a promise. The greeting is the third element of a Greek letter, but the tense has been transformed by Christian truth. The *estai* (will be) of verse 2 has influenced the *estai* of verse 3. The secular form would be a simple greeting (cf. Acts 15:23; James 1:1). The more frequent New Testament form would be in the present tense: "Grace to you and peace . . ." (Galatians 1:3), "Grace, mercy, and peace . . ." (I Timothy 1:2; II Timothy 1:2).

The emphasis on God as Father and on Jesus Christ as the Father's Son is elsewhere expanded into the confession so central in the refutation of the Gnostic denial of this unique relation (cf. I John 2:23). That which may at first seem an awkward addition of "in truth and love" prepares the way for the two major themes in the letter. Love will be discussed first in terms of following the commandment (4-6), then follows the longer part on guarding against the deceivers (7-11). Belief and brotherly love belong together in true Christianity (cf. I John 3:23).

FOLLOWING THE COMMANDMENT: *entolē* (4-6).

4 I rejoiced greatly to find some of your
children following the truth,
just as we have been commanded by the Father.

5 And now I beg you, lady, not as though
I were writing you a new commandment,
but the one we have had from the beginning,
that we love one another.

6 And this is love,
that we follow his commandments;
this is the commandment, as you have heard
from the beginning, that you follow love.

The balance between belief and brotherly love continues. In the salutation, truth was mentioned four times and love twice, but now the proportion is reversed as one verse is given to truth (4) and two to love (5-6). It was the custom for letters to begin with some expression of joy that the sender found in the receivers (cf. III John 3-4; I John 1:1-4; I Thessalonians 1:2; II Thessalonians 1:3; I Cor-inthians 1:4; Romans 1:8; Philippians 1:3; Colossians 1:3). At times the form is that of a blessing (II Corinthians 1:3; Ephesians 1:3; I Peter 1:3). The joy of elder John has a note of sadness, for only "some" of the elect lady's children are following in the path of truth. Others were no doubt following the Gnostic lie, and the report of this, perhaps by traveling brethren, stimulated the letter. Love cannot be separated from truth as truth cannot be separated from love. God the Father commands both. "Love is truth in human action; and truth is love in regard to the order of things" (Westcott).

Following the truth is a Hebrew metaphor for daily conduct. It means literally walking in the truth (cf. I John 1:6-7; 2:6,11; III John 3-4). The formula *en alētheia* (in truth) is now used for the third time (cf. 1, 3), but this is the same truth as that "which abides in us and will be with us forever" (2). The meaning comes out more fully in the refutation of deceivers (7-11). God's command to walk in truth prepares the way for the commandment of love.

Love is expressed in both the singular (commandment, 5) and the plural (commandments, 6), a style noted in other Johannine writings (John 13:34; 14:15; 15:12; I John 2:3-4,7-8; 3:22-24; 5:2-3). Love is so central for the elder that he puts himself in the role of a beggar as he again addresses the elect lady, the local church. The new commandment is the love commandment given by Jesus (John 13:34), so it is really not new. It belongs to the beginning and comes out of eternity, from God (cf. I John 1:1; 2:7,13,14,24; 3:11; John 1:1 for the use of the phrase "from the beginning"). Love for one another is then both old and new (cf. I John 2:7-8). There is nothing in verse 5 that is not in the Fourth Gospel and I John, and it is impossible to understand II John without I John at least. II John supplements I John in an emergency situation.

The plural form makes room for further application (6). This is surely the same style of writing expanded in other places (John 14:15; I John 2:3,4; 3:22,24; 5:2-3). The declarations "this is love" and "this is the commandment" have also many parallels (I John 1:5; 2:25; 3:11,23; 4:3,21; 5:3,4,6,9,11,14,20), another reason for be-lieving that II John presupposes I John. Following Gods' com-

mandments is the same as following love, and the metaphor of
walking is behind the Greek in both cases (cf. 4, III John 3-4).

Walking in love is the same as following the commandments, and
the longer version called keeping the commandments is found in
three long sections of I John (2:3-11; 3:10-24; 4:7-5:3), another
evidence that II John is vitally related to I John. Thus far the letter
has been concerned with *entolē* (commandment), but this is now
followed by *didachē* (doctrine, teaching), an interesting reversal of
the Pauline style of doctrine first and exhortation last.

GUARDING AGAINST THE DECEIVERS: *didachē* (7-11).

7 For many deceivers have gone out into the world,
   men who will not acknowledge the coming of
   Jesus Christ in the flesh;
   such a one is the deceiver and the antichrist.

8 Look to yourselves, that you may not lose
   what you have worked for,
   but may win a full reward.

9 Any one who goes ahead and does not abide
   in the doctrine of Christ does not have God;
   he who abides in the doctrine of Christ
   has both the Father and the Son.

10 If any one comes to you and does not bring this doctrine,
   do not receive him into the house or give him any greeting;

11 for he who greets him shares his wicked work.

The three sections in I John on guarding against the enemy (2:18-
27; 4:1-6; 5:4-11) are now reduced to one. The abrupt change
indicated by the Greek *hoti* (for) has been interpreted by Barclay
to mean: "There is all the more reason to speak like this." This
would have reference to the command to walk in truth and in love
(4-6). The fact that only "some" were following the commandment was reason for the alarm now sounded against false teachings
that were leading others astray.

The false doctrine of the deceivers is described with some of the poetic structure found in I John. The first statement recalls the antichrists in I John 2:19 who went out from the *koinōnia* (fellowship) into the *kosmos* (godless world). It is only on the surface and in a sarcastic manner that these heretics can be described as missionaries (cf. Mark 16:15). They have gone out of the fellowship because they abandoned the true faith (I John 2:19). The real parallel is in I John: "for many false prophets have gone out into the world" (4:1).

The false teaching that denied the true faith is found in the second clause about belief in the flesh of Jesus Christ. A problem of Greek grammar arises when the "has come in the flesh" (perfect tense) of I John 4:2 is compared with the "coming" (present participle) of verse 7. The present participle could have reference to belief in a future coming of Jesus in the flesh, but there is no parallel to such a belief. A statement in the *Epistle of Barnabas* 6:9 has been cited as a parallel to such a belief, but C. H. Dodd is surely correct in his blunt rejection of this view. *Today's English Version* does not violate the Greek with this translation: "Jesus Christ became mortal man." Greek parallels may be found in John 3:31; 6:14; 11:27. The teaching is the same as that rejected in I John 4:1-6.

The third clause is also more detailed in I John 2:18-27. There is nothing new in this verse 7, and the readers would need I John to know the full meaning. Anyone who denies the incarnation of Christ in the flesh of Jesus is "the deceiver and the antichrist."

Those deceived by the deceivers are in danger of losing their full reward (8). The warning is introduced by a formula not found in I John and John, but it has close parallels in other New Testament passages (Mark 13:5,9; Matthew 24:4; Philippians 3:2). What is the full reward (*misthos*) that they are in danger of losing? Bultmann thinks it is the eternal life promised to the faithful (cf. I John 2:55; 5:11-12), but this is not certain. The nearest parallel in the Johannine writings is John 4:36 where *misthos* is used as a parallel to eternal life in the pattern of sowing and reaping. Paul expresses a similar idea with the language of the Greek games (I Corinthians 9:24-27; Philippians 3:12-16). In any case the full reward may be lost by believing the Gnostic lie and living the Gnostic life of sin.

The true doctrine of Christ is the very opposite of the false doctrine of antichrist (9). Unless one accepts C. H. Dodd's view of *chrisma* as doctrine, the concept of *didachē* (doctrine, teaching) is not found in I John, but it is in the Fourth Gospel (7:16-17; 8:19). The Gnostics were the "advanced thinkers" who went on ahead into heresy. Those "deceivers who have gone out into the world" (7) have gone "too far," as Barclay translates *proagōn*. They went so far with the thought forms of paganism that they ended with the content and conduct of pagan theosophy. Johannine theology used many Greek forms, but the content is always apostolic. His doctrine is anchored to the confession found in I John 2:23. It is not possible to have the Father without the Son, for Jesus Christ is "the Father's Son" (3). The truth is so important that it is stated first in the negative, then in the positive.

The prohibition of hospitality to heretics is the only teaching in II John without parallel in I John. This favorite text for heresy hunters may seem harsh to tolerant ears, but the situation in Asia was touch and go (10-11). Irenaeus reports Polycarp's story about John and the Gnostic Cerinthus of Ephesus: "There are also some who heard him relate that John, the disciple of the Lord, went to the baths of Ephesus; and seeing Cerinthus inside he rushed out without taking a bath, saying, 'Let us flee, before the baths fall in, for Cerinthus the enemy of truth is inside'" (*Against Heresies*, III.iii.4).

Hospitality to travelers was very important in the early Christian mission (11. Cf. Matthew 10:14; Luke 10:10; Romans 12:13; Hebrews 13:2; I Peter 4:9). Itinerate prophets depended upon local hospitality as they propagated their views. An early church manual formulated a whole code of conduct for distinguishing between true and false prophets (*Didache*, 11-12). The pagan Greek writer Lucian wrote his *Peregrinus* to expose charlatans who traveled about exploiting Christian communities. In this light the words of the elder are not so harsh, for those who greet false teachers do indeed share in their wicked work. Another side of the picture is seen in the elder's praise of the hospitality of Gaius to true brethren (III John 5-8).

CONCLUSION (12-13).

12 Though I have much to write to you,
   I would rather not use paper and ink,
   but I hope to come to see you and
   talk with you face to face,
   so that our joy may be complete.

13 The children of your elect sister greet you.

The conclusion reveals some interesting things about Greek letter writing. II and III John are about the same length, each being one papyrus page. What were the many things about which he wished to write? If they were an expansion of 5-9, that is to be found in I John; but if in the tone of 10-11, that does not appear until such writings as the *Didache* 11-12. *The New English Bible* speaks of writing in "black and white," but the *Revised Standard Version* translation of "paper and ink" is both literal and clear. A compound of lamp-black and gum was used to write on papyrus, a paper made from Egyptian reeds (cf. III John 3; I Corinthians 3:3).

A personal visit would be more helpful than a letter, so the elder plans to see them in the future (12). *The Revised Standard Version* and *The New English Bible* translations of "face to face" obscure the idiom of "mouth to mouth," drawn perhaps from Numbers 12:8. *The Jerusalem Bible* and *Today's English Version* translations use the adverb "personally" to convey the meaning in modern English. Personal encounter is a way of communication that letters and other indirect media can never equal. In Pogo slang, "eye-ball to eye-ball" is best. The joy of personal fellowship is then restored and made complete (cf. I John 1:4; John 15:11). The elder belongs to one church, but he clearly exercised influence and even authority over the sister church of the readers.

There is now a shift from the plural (12) back to the singular (13) as the church is addressed as an elect sister (cf. 1). The previous shift was from the singular (4-5) to the plural (8,10,12). Only when the church is viewed as a woman does the singular appear. The children are the members of the respective sister churches (cf. I Peter 5:13). Both churches are composed of God's chosen ones, the elect. The sister who sends the greetings is perhaps Ephesus, but the Johannine church which is the receiver is unknown.

The claim of authority from the elder of one church over the members of another church meets with resistance in III John, but it is a resistance more of order than faith. In II John doctrine was the main issue. The two letters are instructive, even if brief, for modern discussions of faith and order face similar situations. It is the insight into early church order that makes II and III John important supplements to the more theological discussions in I John.

Chapter 7

COMMENTARY ON THE THIRD LETTER OF JOHN

SALUTATION TO GAIUS (1-4).

1 The elder to the beloved Gaius,
   whom I love in the truth.

2 Beloved, I pray that all may go well with you
   and that you may be in health;
   I know that it is well with your soul.

3 For I greatly rejoiced when some of the brethren
   arrived and testified to the truth of your life,
   as indeed you do follow the truth.

4 No greater joy can I have than this,
   to hear that my children follow the truth.

This letter also has a sender, a receiver, and a greeting or wish, the usual letter style. Comments on "the elder" and "I love in truth" at II John 1 apply here also, but the receiver of II John was a church while III John is addressed to an individual named Gaius. There was a Gaius of Macedonia (Acts 19:29), a second from Derbe (Acts 20:4), who may be the same as the first if the *The New English Bible* translation of "Doberian" is followed, and still a third in

Corinth (I Corinthians 1:14; Romans 16:23), but this is perhaps a fourth. A. M. Hunter has called him "the Johannine Philemon."[1] It may well be that he is an important layman in the local church (Pergamum or another one in the Johannine circle) in whose home the church met. There is a tradition that John ordained him bishop of Pergamum, but there is no early evidence to support this claim (*Apostolic Constitutions* VII.xl.vi.).

Gaius is called "the beloved," the word found at three other places in this letter (2,5,11) and six times in I John (2:7; 3:2,21; 4:1,7, 11). John the apostle was called the beloved disciple in the Gospel of John (13:23; 19:26; 20:2; 21:7. Cf. 11:3,5). The address is used also by other New Testament writers (I Corinthians 4:14; 10:14; Romans 1:7, I Peter 2:11). It is not enough that Gaius be one who was loved in truth as in the case of the elect lady and her children (II John 1). He must be a very special person in the mind of the elder. Even in the salutation one of the great themes of Johannine teaching is sounded. Johannine Christianity is the way of the new commandment of brotherly love (John 13:34; 14:15; 15:12; I John 2:3-11; 3:11-24; 4:7-5:3; II John 5-6).

The greeting or wish is in the form of a prayer that reveals much about Gaius. He is not only deeply loved by the elder, but his spiritual health is better than his physical condition. It is a rare person who can be so described. This may indicate some physical frailty or temporary illness. The soul is his total well-being, the spirit as well as the body (cf. I Peter 1:9 for the use of the soul in the sense of the total personal life, I John 3:16). The elder is not unconcerned about his physical condition, a concern at times lacking in Gnostic piety that thought only of the spiritual. The idea of prosperity which precedes physical health is used also by Paul (I Corinthians 16:2; Romans 1:10). It means for things to go well. He is also faithful to the apostolic truth (3, cf. II John 1-4). The elder's knowledge of these facts came from traveling brethren who had just arrived (cf. III John 4). The blend of truth and love in Gaius brings a joy like unto that expressed toward the elect lady and her children (cf. II John 4-6). A third statement indicates that he may be a personal convert of the elder, a fact that would rule out identification with any of Paul's converts named Gaius. This would seem

---

[1] *Introducing the New Testament* (London: SCM, 1951), p. 180.

to be the meaning when the elder calls him one of "my children" (4. Cf. I John 2:1,12,28; 3:7,18; 4:4; 5:21). Paul speaks in the same way about converts (I Thessalonians 3:9; Philippians 1:18; Colossians 2:5).

Following the truth is magnified in this greeting (3-4), and this may throw light on the Gnostic heresy in the church. This would rule out the interpretation that the trouble was solely one of division about authority. In the background is heresy as well as schism. Heresy has led to schism. These conclusions cannot be discounted by any claim that these are stylized statements used in a typical letter. There is an old Germany story that proves that Mother Müller is not dead because it was announced in the paper just like other death notices!

COOPERATION OF GAIUS (5-8).

5 Beloved, it is a loyal thing you do
when you render any service to the brethren,
especially to strangers,

6 who have testified to your love before the church.
You will do well to send them on their journey
as befits God's service.

7 For they have set out for his sake
and have accepted nothing from the heathen.

8 So we ought to support such men,
that we may be fellow workers in the truth.

Much more is revealed about Gaius as the elder addresses him again as beloved and calls attention to his attitude toward missionaries sent forth from Ephesus to proclaim the truth in the midst of the Gnostic threat. A rather clear picture is given of the sending and support of missionaries in Asia.

It was in the sending of missionaries that the loyalty and love of Gaius to the elder became manifested. His loyalty or faithfulness enabled him to offer hospitality to Christian brethren even when they were strangers. It was enough that they were the servants of truth. Travel was most difficult for strangers in the ancient world.

Plato the philosopher complained that Greek innkeepers were more like pirates who held their guests for ransom. Guests often paid dearly for miserable accommodations.

Barclay reports that some families in different parts of the country looked after the hospitality of each other's relatives by using a token (*symbolon*) to identify strangers to the host. Large cities had an official called the *Proxenos,* the Greek word for one who looked after strangers. John is applying this practice to the family of God. Fortunately, Christian teachings have penetrated Greek culture enough that in Greece a chain of Xenia, inns for Xenoi (strangers), has now made available in many places comfortable lodging at reasonable rates!

The work of Gaius was more than an act of loyalty to the elder and his missionaries. Most of all it grew out of that love so distinctive in the Johannine teachings (6). A first missionary journey had already been made, and the good report about Gaius was heard before the church (*ekklēsia,* cf. 9), a term not used in I and II John and the Fourth Gospel. Sending one on a journey is the New Testament way to say financial help was given (cf. Acts 15:3; 20:38; 21:5; I Corinthians 16:6; Romans 15:24; Titus 3:13). It is a blessed thing when there are generous Christians of means who put feet on the gospel by providing the means of travel for those who would carry the good news to the ends of the earth. John had his Gaius, and Paul had such friends as Aquila and Priscilla (Acts 18:1-4).

The support of missionaries revealed important relations between Christians and the heathen. Christian missionaries accepted nothing from unbelievers (7). There were good reasons for this practice. Barclay mentions a man who called himself "the slave of the Syrian goddess" who boasted that he never returned from his begging with less than seventy bags of money for his goddess. It was "for his sake" (God's, cf. Acts 5:41) that the early missionaries avoided all practices associated with crooks and quacks (cf. Mark 6:8; Matthew 10:9). They refused to compromise the gospel by campaign contributions! Hospitality was therefore an important issue (Romans 12:13; I Timothy 3:2; 5:9; Titus 1:8; Hebrews 13:2; I Peter 4:9).

The relationship to Christians of means was a very different one (8). The elder claims support for those sent forth. To send (*propempein,* 6) and to support (*hypolambanein,* 8) mean much the same. Those who support those they send are called *synergoi* (fellow workers). This is the word Paul used as a metaphor of the church (I Corinthians 3:9). The elder means those who give and those who go do the work of spreading the truth. That is why hospitality toward heretics was looked upon as participation in the evil work of Gnostic heretics (II John 11, *koinōnei*).

A second missionary journey is now planned. Demetrius with this letter and other missionaries are sent forth to rectify the situation in the church of which Gaius is a member and perhaps other churches in the Johannine circle. They are to be messengers of "the truth" in areas where the Gnostic lie is spreading. It may be possible to translate truth as an adverb, as when *Today's English Version* renders *en alētheia* (in truth) with "truly love" (II John 1:1; III John 1:1), but there seems always to be some of the doctrinal content of the noun (cf. 3-4; II John 1:1-4). It is for John "the truth itself" (12). This is a term later used by Papias of Hierapolis (Eusebius, *Church History*, III.39.3).

OPPOSITION OF DIOTREPHES (9-10).

9 I have written something to the church;
but Diotrephes, who likes to put himself first,
does not acknowledge my authority.

10 So if I come, I will bring up what he is doing,
prating against me with evil words.
And not content with that,
he refuses himself to welcome the brethren,
and also stops those who want to welcome them
and puts them out of the church.

The portrait of the beloved Gaius is followed by one of a domineering Diotrephes. At least three major characteristics stand out in the personality of the elder's stubborn opponent. First of all, he loved the place of pre-eminence (*philoprōteuōn*, 9). The elder had written a previous letter to the church (*ekklēsia* again, cf. 6) that apparently did not set well with Diotrephes. Some have thought this letter to be II John, but none of the early writers thought so. It is more likely a letter now lost that would throw great light on the problem, but the few remarks here are all we know for sure.

The desire of Diotrephes to have first place has caused many to call him the first monarchical bishop, i.e., one who exercised authority over several elders in one local church (cf. I Timothy 3:1; 4:14; 5:17). By the time of Ignatius (c.108) this was the structure of churches in this province of Asia. As such, Diotrephes refused to recognize the authority of the elder whose function in Ephesus was much like that of a metropolitan bishop or archbishop whose authority extended over a group of cities or churches.

Bultmann sums up much German scholarship that tends to see the elder and his missionaries as representatives of a primitive period of charismatic prophets who are now being opposed by a growing institutionalism and legalism in the church, but this is more the echo of Rudolph Sohm's *Kirchenrecht (Church Law,* Vol. 1, 1892; Vol. 2, 1923) than evidence from Scripture and the early church. It is not necessary to revolt as far as Emil Brunner, Hans von Campenhausen, Ernst Käsemann, and others have done to avoid the rigidity of institutionalism. A middle way must be found between Sohm and Rome. Here is a place where British scholarship has been more balanced in judgment.

A second characteristic of Diotrephes was his prating against the elder (10a). The elder himself considers the possibility of a visit to confront the behavior of his opponent. A similar visit was mentioned in II John 12, and this may be used as evidence for the letter of III John 9 being II John, but this is not conclusive. His prating or blabbing *(phlyarōn)* against the elder was uncharitable at least, but some doctrinal differences cannot be ruled out. Authority indeed was the real issue, but there was some reason for the elder to exercise his authority.

The final and perhaps most serious characteristic about Diotrephes was his power in the church (10b). First of all, he refused to welcome the traveling missionaries sent by the elder. The same Greek verb is used for welcoming the brethren as for not acknowledging the elders authority. Gaius was commended for doing this very thing, and he may be the leader of a loyal minority supporting the elder against Diotrephes and the majority in the church. Nothing is said about the excommunication of Gaius, but Diotrephes did have enough power to drive from the church those who would welcome the messengers from the elder. A leader with enough power to dominate the majority in opposition to the elder's authority was a real threat to the unity of the churches, and this explains the urgency of the letter and the possibility of a visit from the elder.

A church schism is clearly in the making. In the case in I John 2:19 the Gnostic heretics were in the minority, so they simply "went out" to form a church in schism. In this other situation there is a major "take over" with the faithful minority driven out (cf. John 9:34-35). What can be done?

EXHORTATION AND RECOMMENDATION OF DEMETRIUS (11-12).

11 Beloved, do not imitate evil but imitate good.
He who does good is of God;
he who does evil has not seen God.

12 Demetrius has testimony from every one,
and from the truth itself;
I testify to him too,
and you know my testimony is true.

For the fourth time Gaius is addressed as the beloved (1,2,5,11). It may be that the strong word of exhortation is to insulate him completely from the evil influence of Diotrephes. To lose this man of means to a usurper would be tragic. Imitation of the evil would be to follow Diotrephes and abandon his previous practice of hospitality to the missionaries sent from the elder of Ephesus.

There is something of a poetic structure to these three lines of moral instruction (11. Cf. II John 6):

Do not imitate evil but imitate good:
whoever does good is of God;
whoever does evil has not seen God.

As imitating evil meant following Diotrephes, so the imitation of the good will in the next verse be represented by Demetrius. Doing good (I John 2:29; 3:6,9) means keeping or following the new commandment of love (I John 2:3-11; 3:11-24; 4:7-21; II John 5-6). This is evidence that one is "of God" (cf. I John 4:1-7 where the phrase is used seven times). Doing evil (I John 3:6,10) is to hate, and this is evidence that one has never "seen God" in Jesus Christ (cf. I John 3:6 where the same verb is used and I John 4:12 where a different verb is used). Is he suggesting that Diotrephes has not "seen God"? Perhaps so.

Demetrius is an example of one who has "seen God" (12). Who is Demetrius? He has been identified with the silversmith of Ephesus who opposed Paul (Acts 19:24). If so, he had a conversion like unto that of Paul! Others have called him the long form of the Demas who forsook Paul but who has now repented and returned (Colossians 4:14; Philemon 24; II Timothy 4:10). This would be pleasant to believe, but it is unlikely. Demetrius, like Gaius, was a common name. He is perhaps the bearer of the letter and the leader of the traveling missionaries. It may be that the elder is sending him to displace Diotrephes as leader in the church. If so, this is an interesting episode in early church policy. There was a fourth century tradition that he was made bishop of Philadelphia as Gaius was made bishop of Pergamum, but this is doubtful *(Apostolic Constitutions,* VII. XLVI).

Demetrius is supported by a threefold testimony (12). Everyone in his church and perhaps all the churches at large spoke well of good Demetrius. Here is another evidence that all Asia looked to the elder as leader. The practice of sending church letters to certify the genuineness of traveling Christians was already established (II Corinthians 3:1; Romans 16:12; Colossians 4:7-8).

Even more, he has the testimony of "the truth itself." This could mean no more than an affirmation that the basis for his good reputation is true, but the Johannine usage means more. Jesus himself is truth in the Gospel of John (14:6) and even the Spirit in I John (5:6). However, in II John (1-4) and III John (1-4,8) the truth is the apostolic faith as opposed to the Gnostic heresy. This is a fifth suggestion that church order and discipline are not the sole reasons for conflict between the elder and Diotrephes (cf. 1,3,4,5,12). The truth itself is the personification of the apostolic faith to which Demetrius had remained faithful in the face of the Gnostic heresy. There is an echo of this personification of truth in the passage from Papias of Hierapolis cited by Eusebius *(Church History,* III 39,3).

The third testimony in favor of Demetrius is that of the elder himself. This includes not only the weight of the elder's position in Asia but all that Gaius had known the elder to be in his defense of the truth against Gnosticism. This is the same type of appeal to

testimony found in the epilogue of the Gospel of John (21:24). The
only testimony greater than that of such a man as the elder is the
testimony of God himself (cf. I John 5:6-12).

CONCLUSION (13-15)

13 I had much to write to you,
   but I would rather not write with pen and ink;

14 I hope to see you soon,
   and we will talk together face to face.

15 Peace be to you.
   The friends greet you.
   Greet the friends,
   every one of them.

The final greetings begin with an echo of words found in the
epilogue of the Gospel of John (20:30), but the motivation is different. In the Gospel the good news about eternal life was of necessity
abbreviated, but now the restraint pertains to trouble in the church.
Only a few stylistic differences are to be found between the final
words of III John 13-14 and those found in II John 12. The "had
much to write" is used for "have much to write" *(eichon for echōn*
and *grapsai* for *graphein)*, the present tense *(thelō)* for past tense
(eboulēthēn) behind "I would," "ink and pen" for "paper and ink"
in Greek (both pen and paper were made of reeds), "I hope to see
you soon" for "I hope to come to you." The Hebrew idiom of
"mouth to mouth" (Numbers 12:8; Jeremiah 39:4) is again the
literal translation of "face to face." The words "that our joy may be
complete" are lacking. An imitator would perhaps have used the
same words in each conclusion, so II and III John must have the
same author.
The last verse has a very personal tone. The "peace to you" is the
normal Jewish *shalom* (cf. John 14:27; I Peter 5:14), but it has a
special meaning for the troubled church. "You" is singular each
time as is the last verb ("greet"), since the elder has Gaius in mind.
"The friends" are the members of the church in Ephesus who add
their greetings to those of the elder. The "every one of them" is
literally "by name," a stylistic way to individualize the greeting.

The *Today's English Version* translation of "personally" and *The New English Bible*, "individually," capture the idiomatic meaning. It would be difficult to be more personal in such a short greeting.

Select Bibliography

Alexander, Neil, *The Epistles of John. Torch Bible Commentaries*. London: SCM Press, 1962.

Barclay, William, *The Letters of John and Jude. The Daily Bible Study*. Philadelphia: Westminster Press, 1958.

Brooke, A. E., *The Johannine Epistles. International Critical Commentary*. Edinburgh: T. & T. Clark, 1912.

Bultmann, Rudolf, *Die drei Johannesbriefe. Meyers Kommentar XIV*. Göttingen: Vandenhoeck & Ruprecht, 1967.

Conner, W. T., *The Epistles of John*. Second and Revised Edition. Nashville: Broadman Press, 1929.

Dodd, C. H., *The Johannine Letters. Moffatt New Testament Commentary*. New York: Harper Brothers, 1946.

Johnston, G., *I, II, III John. Peake's Commentary on the Bible*. London: Thomas Nelson and Sons, 1962.

O'Neill, J. C., *The Puzzle of I John*. London: S.P.C.K., 1966.

Robertson, A. T., *Word Pictures in the New Testament*, Vol. 6. Nashville: Broadman Press, 1933.

Schnackenburg, Rudolf, *Die Johannesbriefe. Herders Kommentar XIII*. Freiburg: Verlag Herder, 1963.

Stott, J. R. W., *The Epistles of John. Tyndale Bible Commentaries*. Grand Rapids: Wm. B. Eerdmans Publishing Company, 1964.

Vawter, Bruce, *The Johannine Epistles. Jerome Biblical Commentary*. Englewood Cliffs, N. J.: Prentice-Hall, 1968.

Westcott, B. F., *The Epistles of John*. London: Macmillan and Company, 1883.

Wilder, Amos N., *The First, Second, and Third Epistles of John. The Interpreter's Bible*, Vol. 12. Nashville: Abingdon Press, 1957.

Williams, R. R., *The Letters of John and James. The Cambridge Bible Commentary*. Cambridge: University Press, 1965.